ODYSSEY OF A WAYWARD TRAVELER

RAYMOND A. UZANAS

authorHOUSE®

Raymond Uzanas was born on May 1, 1942, in Hartford, CT. A former president and CEO of Amplex Corp., he continues to enjoy adventure travel throughout the world. Ray lives in the seaside village of Stonington, CT.

AuthorHouse™
1663 Liberty Drive, Suite 200
Bloomington, IN 47403
www.authorhouse.com
Phone: 1-800-839-8640

First published by AuthorHouse 6/18/2008

ISBN: 978-1-4343-2487-0 (sc)
ISBN: 978-1-4343-2488-7 (hc)

Library of Congress Control Number: 2007905577

Printed in the United States of America
Bloomington, Indiana

This book is printed on acid-free paper.

Photographs by author.

Song of the Open Road

"Afoot and lighthearted,
I take to the open road.

Healthy, free, the world before me,
leading wherever I choose.

Henceforth, I ask not good fortune,
I myself am good fortune.

Henceforth, I whimper no more,
postpone no more, need nothing.

Strong and content,
I travel the open road."

Walt Whitman

DEDICATION

To my mother Genevieve, who many years ago encouraged me to see as much of the United States as possible. She loved this country and all it stood for and wanted me to experience that same appreciation. She was so right.

CONTENTS

Introduction   1

Preparation   7

Leg One: South And Southeast   11

Leg Two: Southwest   57

Leg Three: West, Northwest   93

Leg Four: Eastward Bound   135

Epilogue   187

Acknowledgements   193

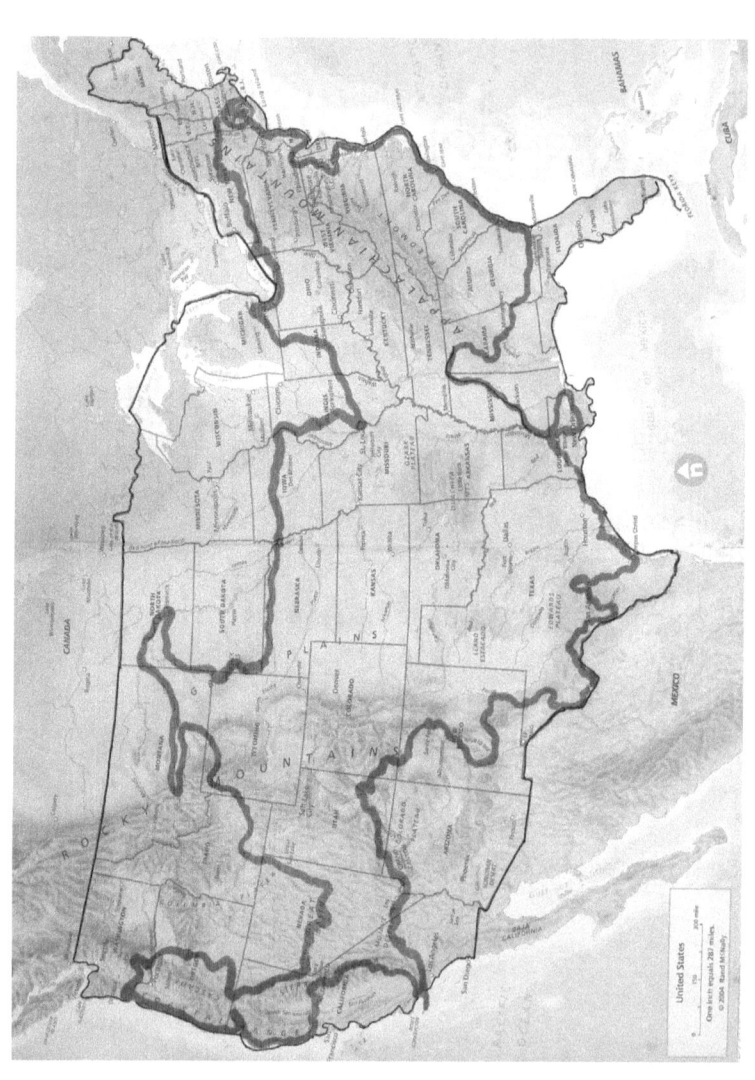

INTRODUCTION

When asked by friends why I would sell my beautiful seaside home in the resort village of Watch Hill, RI, and with minimal planning head out across the U.S.A. alone for an indeterminate length of time, my short answer was: "so I can figure out what I want to do when I grow up." As I was sixty-two years old at the time, I did not think my answer was convincing, but it was succinct and reasonably accurate. I would embark on a journey of self discovery and adventure as a homeless traveler. A condominium in the fishing village of Stonington, CT, to which I was committed to buy, would not be ready for occupancy for another eighteen months; there was much uncertainty over where I would reside until then.

Inadvertently, the seeds of my journey were planted in April 2004 when I traveled with my three grandsons to the Galapagos Islands. It was an exciting and memorable experience for all of us and my first extended trip in many years.

Until my wife Loretta was diagnosed with bone marrow cancer in 1992, she and I enjoyed adventure traveling to many of the wild regions of the world. These activities ceased as her extensive medical treatments (including a bone marrow transplant, radical mastectomy, and various surgeries and chemotherapies) dominated our lives up to her death the evening of June 17, 2003. During the same period we shared the

1

affections of three cocker spaniel siblings, Adamas, Buffy, and Buster, all of whom had to be put to rest within the twelve month period surrounding Loretta's death. While the Galapagos foray was intended to provide a rich educational experience to the boys, for me it was more. In my walks around the islands, Loretta seemed omnipresent; after all, she had been my constant traveling companion since our teens. I lacked that intimate partner to share the experience. I needed to internalize and savor these opportunities of personal growth.

I always had a passion for travel, starting with my family's modest getaways during my youth in the 1950s. My father was an upholsterer, worked long hours, and time off from his work was precious and hard to come by. A typical vacation away from our home was taken in July and lasted for three or four days. For example, one in 1953 was to Niagara Falls and included visits to Howe Caverns and Cooperstown as well as the Catskills, where a popular animal game farm was located. With my younger sister Doris in the back seat of our 1950 Plymouth Belvedere, I was enthralled by the scenery on our drive through New York's Finger Lakes region, much different than that surrounding our tenement apartment in Hartford's racially diverse North End. I recall the sadness I felt when we would arrive back home. Despite returning to my friends and endless hours of sandlot baseball, I wanted to see more of our country. The following year we motored to Washington D.C. for a few days, and the same feelings emerged.

Fast forwarding to the 1960s and 70s, I now had a wife and three children. Our family vacations were modest and more frequent, this made possible because we bought a "pop up" (tent) trailer. It afforded us the opportunity to travel often and cheaply, and we did this throughout the eastern United States and Canada. I loved it, seeing new places and especially spending time outdoors. Loretta was a great sport and companion; as long as there was a visit to a major league baseball park in our plans, our son Steve enjoyed the trips as well. His younger sisters, Cher and Chris, separated in age by little more than a year, were constant companions and enjoyed doing most anything. Those times were precious to me and remain some of my fondest memories.

During that period, I found employment with a start up company (Amplex Corp.) in the industrial diamond business, about which I knew nothing. My position was advertised as a laboratory trainee, but as I was their second employee (low person on the totem pole), packaging, shipping and other mundane tasks occupied the majority of my time early on. My university studies would have to continue part time as I needed to provide for our family's financial needs.

The diamond business is international in scope; as our company and my stature grew and our influence in the diamond markets increased, my opportunities for visiting other regions, stateside and overseas, similarly increased. My travels were taking me throughout Europe and Asia, and I always included Loretta on my post-business trips abroad. On our own, or with others, we enjoyed vacations to many of the exotic places around the globe. Safaris to Africa, treks through Southeast Asian and Central American jungles, and several sailing cruises in the Caribbean proved unforgettable.

All this came to an abrupt halt with Loretta's unexpected and shocking cancer diagnosis in November 1992, a few days shy of Thanksgiving Day: multiple myeloma, defined as "a universally fatal, B-cell malignancy." Everything changed! Traveling was difficult for Loretta as her myeloma treatments and the aftermath left her with little energy. A later breast cancer diagnosis and the ensuing treatments further detracted from her quality of life. To Loretta's credit, she redirected her time and effort toward designing, making, and selling floral arrangements. These activities, which she continued until her final year, often required Herculean efforts.

Now, after twelve years of very limited travel, had my wanderlust waned? I felt my energy level was high and I continued to be blessed with good health to pursue active travel. But did I want to anymore? While limited in recreational traveling during Loretta's illness, I maintained an active sport regimen, which included surf casting and salt water fly fishing for striped bass and bluefish from the Watch Hill beaches.

I was an active member and enthusiastic golfer at Stonington Country Club, which Loretta and I had joined before there was a golf course on site. I practiced and played often while achieving a reasonable level of competence (mid- to high- single-digit handicap). Interestingly, Loretta also had a passion for golf, albeit with a high handicap; but she remains to this day the only one of us to have scored a "hole-in-one"! And don't think this wasn't a source of some good natured teasing when I got a bit too pompous in my critiques of her swing mechanics.

Nonetheless, upon returning from the Galapagos, it was exceedingly clear to me that my thirst for travel remained unquenched. Thoughts of seeing more of this "wonderful world," as Louis Armstrong so eloquently put it to music, were enticing me. There was also the matter of moving forward as a widower whose entire adulthood and part of adolescence was spent in a forty-three year union with his high school sweetheart.

In a magazine article I came across there were five questions given to participants in a training exercise at one of the Fortune 100 companies:

> 1) If you were on your deathbed and wanted to tell your children or the young people to whom you are close the three most important things you have learned in life, what would they be?
> 2) What gives you the greatest joy, satisfaction, and renewal in your life?

3) Who are you without your job, your money?

4) What activities could you add to your life that would be a source of richness and joy?

5) Think of someone you deeply admire and why.

I wanted to provide answers, not only for my benefit but especially for my family, since these are the kinds of answers which I want to be part of my legacy. The solitude, observations, and interactions along my journey provided a nourishing environment for me to contemplate these questions. Whether during a chance encounter in a pre-Revolutionary town in Virginia, at a campground in West Texas, climbing the canyon lands of Utah, following portions of the Lewis and Clark Trail, hiking in the Eden-like valleys of Yellowstone, or touring the Lincoln Museum in Springfield, IL, I found myself immersed in areas so special that they conjured up answers from deep within.

My journey was multifaceted: an opportunity to see and experience much of what our country and its people are all about, a challenge to my own resources in managing the issues that traveling alone in unfamiliar places brings, and an opportunity to examine my character as honestly as possible in order to better understand who I am and where I want to go with my life.

Being apart from family members and friends was not easy, although this difficulty was mitigated with modern technologies such as cell phones, satellite phones, and e-mail. These devices, however, do not substitute for the loss of personal time that I would have shared with many who mean so much to me. This was the journey of a wayward traveler.

PREPARATION

My odyssey would begin after the closing sale of my home. This decision reflected my intent to embark on my trip free of material or related distractions that could divert my focus. While I credited myself with a penchant for compartmentalizing issues of my personal and professional life, I nonetheless needed to separate myself, however briefly, from the memories of eighteen Watch Hill years. Thus, with no permanent living quarters for the duration of my trip, I kept clothes and personal artifacts not accompanying me in a local self storage facility to be accessed as required.

A decision had to be made about my mode of transportation. What vehicle would I consider most appropriate for this trip? I considered a van or camper, but I quickly dismissed that idea as I was not interested in spending every night so confined or being restricted in any off road drives. I decided on a crossover (SUV on an auto chassis) vehicle that would provide adequate interior space; all-wheel drive for off road driving and/or bad road conditions; and a multitude of creature-comfort, convenience features. My 2005 Cadillac SRX included a GPS navigation system and On Star satellite service, so I didn't exactly "rough it"!

Another issue was communications and how I would keep in contact with family, friends, and associates during my travels. Current technology proved to be both a blessing and a curse. Nowadays, maintaining contact is much easier than back when John Steinbeck traveled with Charlie in 1960.

I purchased an IBM laptop computer, which was the easy part; but it was a challenge to find the best way to connect to internet sites along my route. I don't mean this to be a treatise on what is the current state of our communication technology, but my experience suggests that inconsistency in the use and availability of these technologies across our country is readily apparent, and the various ways of connecting to the internet in 2005 were frustrating and annoying. In fairness I should add that my computer skills are minimal; my success with it may be akin to what a purple belt karate student (which is as far as I got) might enjoy in a confrontation with Chuck Norris.

Also, with much of my time spent in outlying regions, especially in the western parts of our country, cell phone service was sporadic. In a few instances, mostly in areas surrounded by mountains or canyons, neither could the On Star satellite phone pick up a signal. That is surprising unless one realizes the "satellite" feature is only for the guidance portion of the system, a point salespeople were not at pains to make clear.

My travel inventory included golf clubs, fly fishing rod and accessories, pup tent, sleeping bag and associated camp gear, clothing and shoes, cameras, binoculars, portable CD player, blankets, rain gear, laptop computer, cell phone, and a CB radio. The latter was a gift to me by a friend and proved to be a source of comfort and safety as I took it on my solo hikes in some remote areas where my only means of communication was via this device. I assembled a collection of books and other travel materials garnered from a variety of places that would serve as guides, and several non-fiction audio books chosen with a view to my anticipated destinations.

Finally and most importantly, I needed a reliable and trustworthy person to administer the details of my personal finances that would have to be overseen during my absence. This vital task was entrusted to my sister. I could never overestimate the value of having Doris handle my week to week finances while I was away.

I was blessed with the full support of my family, including my mother, who turned eighty-eight years old in February of that year. Mom had been living in an assisted care facility in Connecticut and I would see her regularly and speak with her often, but I wasn't sure how she would react to my being gone for long periods. As it happened, her continued enthusiastic responses to my adventures were precious and much appreciated.

I had no pre-planned route and seasonal climatic conditions naturally played a major role in determining my direction of travel. Since departure was in January, my weather sensitive route began from the eastern shores and through the southern border states. I noted on my map the locations of the national parks, as well as a few other sites I wanted to visit. At the same time, I made a conscious effort to bypass regions that I'd visited previously, as well as major cities (with a few exceptions) and interstate highways (whenever plausible). Whatever I saw or routes I took would be determined while I was in the area. The flexibility to adopt such an indeterminate itinerary was facilitated by the fact I was traveling alone and with no particular time constraints.

Leg One: South And Southeast

After several farewell lunches and dinners with family and friends, and following the closing on my home sale, my wayward adventure across the U.S.A. officially began. I left Watch Hill on January 5, 2005, driving south along the New Jersey coast to see my son Steve and his wife Marla in Cape May. I don't get to see them often, both because of the driving distance and the demands of Steve's job as a morning DJ and program director of a popular Atlantic City radio station. It was a heartwarming visit with the two of them and the next morning, after a loving farewell, I continued to Washington, DC, to visit an acquaintance, Myrna, who I'd recently met through the sale of my home. Her family, in fact, are its new owners.

Fig. 1 - A final farewell to Watch Hill, RI residence

I arrived late morning at her palatial home in the embassy section of Washington, DC. Having barely survived the nightmarishly snarled traffic of the downtown, I would have welcomed most any destination, but this one truly set a standard of elegance. If one imagined a smaller version of the Vanderbilt's *Breakers* mansion in Newport, RI, this was it.

After a tour of Myrna's posh home and surroundings, we enjoyed lunch at her favorite Georgetown eatery. Bidding her a grateful goodbye, I continued to the Maryland shore on my way to Cambridge for the evening, passing through Oxford, a sleepy little eastern shore town, formerly a port-of-entry into colonial Maryland. While driving about the area, I passed a home that advertised "goose picking" with a simple sign on the front lawn. This service is provided to successful hunters to pluck their birds' feathers. The area attracts a large migratory bird population, which during hunting season keeps the "pluckers" very busy.

The following morning a fifty-minute drive south from Cambridge took me to the Blackwater National Wildlife Refuge where I purchased a National Park Service Golden Age Passport, available to anyone sixty-two years or older. For a onetime fee of ten dollars it grants the cardholder (and all occupants of his/her vehicle) lifetime, free admission to all U.S. national parks as well as discounted rates for related park services such as campground fees. Considering the extensive time I expected to spend throughout our national parks, the savings alone promised to pay for several fill ups for my gas guzzling SUV.

Blackwater Refuge in winter was special. The deciduous trees and shrubs had shed their leaves, permitting optimum viewing of the landscape and the abundant wildlife, including Bald Eagles, Blue Herons, and Red-Tail Hawks. I continued on to Assateague Island National Refuge at the extreme end of Maryland's eastern shore. I was able to view the wild ponies and deer while enjoying 65° F temperatures. The ponies readily approached my car, sticking their heads in the open driver's window looking for food handouts, and only backing away when their efforts proved unsuccessful. Unauthorized feeding of these animals by tourists has contributed to this habit, which is not healthy either for the animals or the person feeding them and is strongly discouraged by warning signs and applicable fines.

The next day was one of the most fulfilling of my journey and a precursor to what at least part of this trip would be about. Very early the following morning I left the small town of Accomac for a leisurely drive south to the Chesapeake Bay Bridge Tunnel. I stopped at the village of Eastville, which was little changed from Revolutionary days. There were a few remaining federal style buildings in a town of fewer than a thousand residents. I got out of my car to take a few photos of the restored and preserved buildings along the main street. It was then I noticed a weather-beaten shack with an open door and an equally weather-beaten man, sitting in a chair with a pipe showing through his disheveled beard. I crossed the street, camera in hand, and politely introduced myself to this man who had been watching my every move. He was most cordial and shared with me his knowledge of Eastville, past and present, but with little enthusiasm. This area continues to be one of the poorest in the region. The principal business is tomato growing. Well into our conversation, Henry commented on my new car, at which point I informed him it was currently my home as well as my transportation. When he expressed disbelief, I shared with him some of my background as to what brought me here. As I recollected my life's turns over the past couple of years with Loretta's passing, Henry's eyes widened and he listened intently to what I was saying.

What followed could best be described as an act of divine intervention as he proceeded to relate his own personal struggles coming to grips with the loss of his wife of 57 years. Coincidentally, his wife died June 17, 2004, one year to the day after Loretta's death. His questions as to how I got through the first year led to a dialogue that lasted an hour and a half, and he freely poured out his sorrow and frustration in trying to cope with his loss. His queries continued, as did my own questions for him. My responses seemed to encourage him and nourish both of us as I revisited my first year, post- Loretta challenges and the personal emptiness that was tempered with relief that her sufferings had ended. I sincerely believe our discussion led Henry to acknowledge there was hope to ease the anguish he had been feeling the past six months, and that he would be able to move forward. This was a particularly gratifying experience for me and, coming at the start of the trip, raised my spirits immeasurably.

Fig. 2 - Henry the furniture refinisher, Eastville, VA

After a sincere farewell to Henry, I crossed the Chesapeake Bay Bridge into Norfolk, VA. It was a balmy 75 degrees and ideal for a tour of the U.S.S. Wisconsin, an Iowa class battleship with service in World War II, the Korean Conflict, and the Gulf War. I followed that with a visit to the General Douglas MacArthur Memorial and the museum complex. General MacArthur and his wife's remains are interred here, as Norfolk was the home of his mother. With the near perfect weather continuing, I took a lengthy walk around town for the rest of the afternoon, eventually checking into the historic *Clarion James Madison Hotel,* an ideally located downtown hotel, past its best days, but nonetheless attractive with its dark woodwork interior and charming décor.

Late that afternoon I visited the Chrysler Art Museum, near downtown Norfolk. The impressive, spacious building displayed over 30,000 objects once the property of Walter Chrysler, founder of the automobile company bearing his name, and builder of New York's

Chrysler Building. The collection spans 4,000 years of history and includes a world renowned glass collection, especially rich in pieces of L.C. Tiffany.

I departed Norfolk at daybreak driving past the Great Dismal Swamp on my way to Kitty Hawk, NC, for a visit to the Wright Brothers Memorial, the museum and the actual (unchanged) site of their first flight, covering 120 feet in 12 seconds. This was a pleasant two-hour regression into aviation history and one of many places I visited on my journey that highlighted accomplishments made possible by the will, patience, and persistence of many of our fellow countrymen.

Fig. 3 - Original runway for Orville Wright's first flight, Kitty Hawk, NC

Passing Nags Head, I stopped at Jockey Ridge State Park, site of the highest sand dunes on the east coast. I became disoriented while hiking the 120 ft. dunes since there were no nearby objects to lend a perspective on distances and it was surprising how far I had to walk to the summit.

What initially looked like a cakewalk turned out to be much more as the compressed distances seen from below gave way to the reality of much greater expanses along the walk. From there I continued to Cape Hatteras and its famous lighthouse, twenty-five miles south. I stopped briefly to photograph the tallest (208 ft. high) brick lighthouse in the U.S.A. before driving to the Ocracoke Island ferry.

The rapid deterioration in the weather with heavy, wind-driven rains caused a two-hour delay in the ferry's departure. By the time I arrived on Ocracoke, the ferry leaving for the mainland was closed for the day. I found overnight accommodations at *Blackbeard's Inn*, named for the notorious 18th century pirate who met his demise off Ocracoke's coast. That evening I had time to think about my drive along the Outer Banks, a flat spit of barrier islands off the North Carolina coast. I was amazed at the number of homes on stilts along the shoreline; many were valued at well over one million dollars. It seems to me that one intense storm with a tsunami-like wave could wash everything into the ocean. It reminded me of an oversized Napatree Point in Watch Hill waiting for that 1938 hurricane. Yet the building boom continues.

I arrived early the next morning at the ferry terminal, but at that point the ferry was still shut down because wind speeds were exceeding thirty knots. It was well after daybreak before the captain elected to depart, a decision for which I was grateful. After the ferry docked at Cedar Island, I continued to Wilmington, NC, detouring for a drive through Camp Lejeune, the 100,000- acre U.S. Marine base established during WWII.

Further on I stopped at the community of Holly Ridge, the "Venus Flytrap Capital of the World" to search for and photograph this elusive insect- devouring plant. The flytrap species, which Charles Darwin called "the most wonderful plant in the world," does not grow wild in any part of the world, except within a seventy-five mile radius of Wilmington.

Knowing that fact is one thing, but locating these diminutive carnivores is another challenge. My efforts to find one in the wild were tedious, time consuming, and unsuccessful. Frustrated, I stopped for lunch at a roadside diner where I spotted a police car in the lot. I saw two state trooper/wildlife officers having lunch inside and I approached them inquiring where I could find a Venus flytrap. I was abruptly informed it was illegal to remove these plants from their habitat. When I told them that I only wanted to photograph a specimen or two, the response was "good luck finding one"! Persisting in the face of what seemed like indifference on their part, I asked if there were areas nearby that might be worth checking out. One of the officers said there was a state forest just up the road where the plants were numerous but then reminded me of the difficulty in spotting them. Apparently they are small, with a ground cover-like growth habit, and likely to be covered this time of year with leaves and other plant debris. But I was determined.

I left the diner just after the troopers. As I was getting into my car, one of them said to follow them. I did, not knowing what to expect, but soon we entered the forest reserve where we trekked on foot among mounds of moist pine bogs. And lo and behold! Atop the damp moss, rust colored this time of year, were several patches of small, bright green, spike-laden leaves of the Venus flytrap. I gently removed a sparse covering of dead pine needles and photographed the specimens, while again being reminded it is a crime to remove these plants from their growing sites.

After acknowledging their assistance, I departed the area and proceeded past the glitz of Myrtle Beach and through the fishing village and harbor marina of Murrells Inlet to Georgetown, settled in 1526 and considered the first European outpost in North America. At one time it was a rice plantation center. It is now home to a steel and paper mill.

The weather was cold, raw, and windy as I dined that evening at a local favorite, *Thomas Cafe*, enjoying their Low Country crab cake special. The following day was my first Sunday on the road and I thought it important to attend church, give thanks to God, and pray that my journey continued to go well. A short walk from my inn was the Prince George Winyah Episcopal Church, established in 1721. I was heartily welcomed by the very friendly congregation and I savored my reflective moments during the service. With few exceptions my approach to this journey seems to have been somewhat cautionary, mechanical, and introversive. Perhaps learning to be a wayward traveler requires a little experience, a little getting used to.

My next destination was Charleston, SC, where I first stopped at Patriot Point and toured the U.S.S. Yorktown aircraft carrier, as well as a Coast Guard vessel and destroyer. The afternoon was very windy and cold when I boarded a ferry to Fort Sumter in Charleston Bay, where the first shots of the Civil War were fired on April 12, 1861. Despite disagreeable weather, I toured the partially restored fort, its courtyard, and surroundings, including the museum containing numerous Civil War artifacts. Cannons positioned around the perimeter of the fort were the main heavy artillery of those times, and a park guide gave an excellent presentation on their technology and use.

In Charleston I checked into the elegant *John Rutledge House*, a converted 1763 residence, for a two-night stay. After watching the New England Patriots annihilate the Indiana Colts in their NFL playoff game, I dined at *Hanks*, a trendy seafood restaurant in downtown Charleston. The friendliness of the staff and customers validated Charleston's reputation as the "friendliest city in the United States" and it was a fun evening with plenty of social bantering among the largely yuppie and X-generation patrons. The following morning started out cold and windy with wind chill readings in the upper teens, but it was a sunny clear day, ideal for a brisk walk about town. I had a brochure showing the locations of various historic homes; since it was before their 10:00 opening, I enjoyed a vigorous two- hour walk through the central parts of the city.

Of the many mansions and plantations I toured in Charleston, one that stood out and resonated for me was an urban plantation, *Ashton Rhett*, operated by the Preservation Society, whose mission is to preserve, not restore, the structure and grounds. Everything remained as it was in the 1860s, from the grand ballroom in total disrepair, to the dank, bare slave quarters. Coincidentally, while I was touring the mansion's slave quarters, directly below me was a parade forming to honor Dr. Martin Luther King, as it was the holiday celebrating his life.

It was my first visit to Charleston. My initial impression on entering the city was that it didn't overwhelm me with any particular aspect of its heritage or culture. However, once within its core and having familiarized myself with its layout and amenities, I came to appreciate Charleston's historical significance, the architectural beauty of its homes and public buildings, its manicured and inviting parks, and especially its friendly people. Charleston was a wonderful place to visit and may be an even better, albeit it costly, place to live.

I left early the next morning in 22-degree weather under clear sunny skies, looking forward to visiting *Middletown Place* and *Drayton Hall,* two antebellum plantations a short ride from Charleston. Traveling through the South had stimulated my interest in the sociology of pre- and post-Civil War periods, and it seemed to me the most revealing evidence of those times was found in the plantations. The National Trust and another private, non-profit foundation now administer these properties and provide visitors with a meaningful sense of the lives of slaves and masters during that era.

Drayton Hall, built in 1742, was one of twenty plantations (mostly rice) owned by John Drayton, and when it was turned over to the National Trust in 1974, it still lacked plumbing and heating. The preserved mansion with bare-boned rooms, absent furnishing or décor of any kind, provided a window into the history of the house and family. It was a frigid day and the unheated mansion discouraged our group of four visitors from languishing.

Middletown Plantation was a more active place with its extensive English gardens and tours of both the home and slave quarters, which were recreated since most of the original buildings were burned by the Union army. It was the plantation's story of slave life that most stood out. A tour and lecture by a knowledgeable guide provided an in-depth description of the "task system" whereby the slaves were assigned a job that had to be completed before attending to their own family's work. Extensive written records were on site, noting when each slave was bought and sold and for how much.

Continued cold weather dampened my enthusiasm for spending more time enjoying an extensive walk in the gardens. As I continued south to Beaufort, SC, the temperature warmed up nicely and I enjoyed a pleasant walk about this charming coastal town. Several older, stately homes dotted the area near the waterfront. A couple of blocks into town, I visited the *Rhett House Inn*, a charming mansion turned B&B that was the filming site for the movie *Prince of Tides* with Barbara Streisand.

Nearby was a memorial site honoring one of Beaufort's most famous citizens, Robert Smalls. Born into slavery in 1839, he eventually became a captain in the U.S. Navy and later served five terms in the U.S. House of Representatives. After leaving Congress, Smalls was duty collector for the port of Beaufort where he died in 1916. His burial site at Beaufort's Baptist Tabernacle Church is marked with his bust noting his accomplishments.

Leaving Beaufort in the late afternoon, I arrived in Savannah, GA, toward darkness and checked into a local hotel along the river walk in the historical area of town. I dined that evening at a highly recommended popular local restaurant *Lady and Two Sons*, owned and operated by the now famous Paula Deen, and specializing in southern fried chicken, well worth all its accolades. Savannah greeted me on my early morning walk with sunny skies and below freezing temperatures. As I walked along the waterfront, there were two dolphins swimming up river. I enjoyed their antics and learned it was not unusual to have dolphins in this section of the river.

I spent the rest of the morning on a walking tour of Savannah, before heading south to Midway, founded in 1754 by a band of Puritans, two of whom (Lyman Hall and Button Guinett) signed the Declaration of Independence. My visit included a tour of the 200-year-old Midway Church with its original pulpit and slave gallery intact. The adjacent plantation was home to a family who lived there and chronicled their lives before, during, and after the Civil War in an extensive collection of letters among family members. Many of the letters were subsequently compiled into a book format and later published under the title *Children of Pride*.

It was late in the day and my emerging adventuresome spirit led me to bypass the comfort of a motel in favor of Hostel-in-the-Forest, a unique hostel I'd read about in my most oft-referenced travel book, *Road Trip USA*, a treasure chest of information covering a wide swath of interesting and off- beat places to be discovered along the two-lane highways of America.

A mile into the forest was a compound consisting of a common building, several smaller structures (such as outhouses, hen house, chicken coop, and a dozen tree huts), and wooden structures 15 feet up the pine trees via an attached ladder. My hut was rudimentary, dimly lit, but artistically decorated by its previous occupants. The bed and coverings were basic yet comfortable and warm. Dinner that evening consisted of homemade vegetable soup, salad, and chopped beef with vegetables in pita bread, all of it very good. The hostel was staffed by varying numbers of people, depending on the season and available personnel, and it is meant to be a refuge for travelers staying anywhere from one night, as I did, up to several months. In the case of longer stays guests help out with the running of the facility and other aspects of the operation, including construction of additional buildings. Before dinner, we all gathered around an open fire in a great circle giving thanks for our day and what brought us there. Dinner was served on picnic tables in an outside screened room. My contribution to the preparation and clean up efforts was washing the dishes from our twelve-person gathering, which I did enthusiastically in appreciation for the dinner and accommodation cost of fifteen dollars. I retired to my hut and was in my sleeping bag fast asleep by 9:30.

Hostel-in-the-Forest has been around for thirty years and was started by a local lawyer who was interested in the outdoors and travel. The largest of the cabins contains a common room and adjacent sleeping areas for a transient staff of six to ten persons. Also located on the extensive grounds is a lake and river with simple but functional rafts and canoes available. Artistry of all types abounds everywhere. An ingeniously-designed hot tub built along the pathways to the lake, the paintings and sculpturing throughout the buildings, and most especially an extensive manmade labyrinth adjacent to the main building epitomize the artistry and creativity of the staff as well as that of the visitors to this site. According to staffers, Hostel-in-the-Forest has been fertile ground for some visitors to meet their future spouses.

Fig. 4 – Ever-changing labyrinth created by guests and staff of Hostel-in-the-Forest, Brunswick, GA

The following day began with me being startled awake at 4:00 a.m. by the sounds of crowing roosters stalking about beneath my tree hut. Given the rudimentary construction of the bed and mattress, I slept surprisingly well until the fowl members of our community announced their presence. After an early morning exploratory walk in the area, I continued toward Georgia's barrier islands, finally arriving for dinner and lodging at the landmark *Jeckyll Island Club Hotel*, formally the haunt of our country's business titans in the early 1900s. Now into the 21st century, this centerpiece of the Georgia- owned Jeckyll Island remains an impressive place. In between, on a warm, sunny day, I drove around the small, manicured, and charming island; walked the beach; and played a round of golf at the Indian River Course. As I'd not played any golf for several months, my generously carded score of

83 was respectable. As it turned out, I was not tempted onto another golf course for almost three months.

Early on the 21st of January, where back home the weather was a frigid 5° F, I left for St. Mary's to board the National Park Service ferry to Cumberland Island, formerly the private enclave of the Carnegie family at the turn of the 20th century. Now a nature preserve, it is serene and beautiful in its natural makeup of sea, marsh, and forest of 400 year old live oaks and it abounds with wild horses and turkeys. The Carnegie family mansion, *Greyfield*, is currently operated by their heirs as an upscale lodge and restaurant. JFK Jr. was married in the island's tiny twelve-seat African Baptist Church.

Under a bright blue sky with temperatures in the eighties, I hiked along the driftwood laden trails leading to the beach where the sun's rays and soft sand beach afforded me the ideal setting for a mid-afternoon nap. The expansive white sand beach and blue ocean waters reminded me of the beautiful beaches of Watch Hill where Loretta and our family spent innumerable days frolicking in the crashing surf, sand sculpturing, and otherwise enjoying its beauty and tranquility.

After the 45-minute ferry ride to the mainland, I drove to Folsom, GA, a small town near the entrance to the Okefenokee National Wildlife Refuge. I booked a room for the evening and looked forward to spending a full day visiting the interior of the swamp. Dinner that evening was at a homey, local eatery, where I savored the freshest, juiciest fried oysters imaginable; a dinner-size plate cost seven dollars! Incredible! The next day was all Okefenokee Swamp. First, at a national refuge area outside Folsom I took a two-hour boat tour. There was an abundance of Sandhill cranes and other water birds and a few alligators along our route amid the primeval landscape of Okefenokee.

Fig. 5 - Tranquil winter beauty among the cypress of Okefenokee Swamp, Folsam, GA

In the afternoon I drove for an hour to the western side of the refuge to the Steven Foster State Park, named for the songwriter who penned "Old Folks at Home." It is this western end where the water reservoir gives rise to the Suwannee River. Once again I enjoyed the two-hour boat ride four miles into the swamp along cypress-studded watery pathways with many alligators. The bare trees afforded an open look at the swamp and its inhabitants. The large number of tall, moss-draped cypress trees reflected their images in the clear, black waters of the ancient swamp.

I arrived in the town of Valdosta to spend the evening and appreciated my full day at Okefenokee even more since the temperature the following day dropped into the 30s after being well into the 60s. As I lamented the one-day cold spell, New England (especially its southeastern coast) was being bombarded that twenty-third of January with the blizzard of 2005. Watch Hill received two feet of new snow!

After attending Sunday services at a Methodist church in Valdosta, I drove north to Warm Springs, GA, site of the Little White House where FDR often conducted the business of government and died April 12, 1945, while having his portrait painted. The unfinished portrait remains on the premises. President Roosevelt originally went there because of the warm, mineral-laden springs that he felt were therapeutic for his polio. He ultimately established a treatment center there for polio victims who might also benefit from exercising in the 88° F spring waters. After a tour of the wooden three-bedroom retreat and small adjacent museum, I enjoyed a light lunch at a café in the quaint village of Warm Springs.

The following day's hour-and -a-half ride to Montgomery was shortened after crossing into Alabama's central standard time zone, thus gaining me an extra hour. I arrived at the Visitor's Center and watched a video tour of Montgomery before boarding a trolley for a tour of the city.

I wanted to better understand the racially motivated events that took place in and around Montgomery during the tumultuous 1960s. I was fortunate to meet a black trolley driver, Bob, who was about my age and raised in Montgomery, which gave him firsthand insight into the civil rights movement in that area. I was the sole rider on the trolley for two hours while we toured the city and openly and candidly shared our views on the subject. He used the following analogy to describe the difficulty an outsider may have in understanding those events. Consider a football game; some will view the game on a tv screen, and others will see it from the stadium seating. A smaller group will observe the action from the sidelines as non-participating supporters; and finally, there are the players on the field. His point was that the intensity and understanding of the civil rights movement varied with the perspective of the observer.

For his part as an on field participant, he saw a less bellicose Governor George Wallace, who was raised in a predominately black neighborhood and had to play by the rules of the southern segregationists to keep his authority. When I asked why Governor Wallace in three elections received more than 60 percent of the black vote, Bob's response was: "the black community would rather know the devil in office"!

I really enjoyed Bob's company and appreciated his recollections of the civil rights movement of the 1960s. On my own I visited the state capitol building where Jefferson Davis was sworn in as the president of the Confederacy, the same steps on which Governor Wallace in 1965 vigorously defended segregation. Ironically, the Dexter Street King Baptist Church where Martin Luther King was minister from 1954 to 1960 is a stone's throw from those same steps. Interestingly, Dr. King's Montgomery residence was a ten-minute walk from that of Governor Wallace.

My visit to the Rosa Parks Museum was poignant, especially the featured exhibit, which recreated the famous scene where she refused to give up her seat on the bus. Using a cutout bus model with cleverly imposed video footage, this action scene gave one a sensitive understanding of that moment in our country's civil rights history.

The nearby Civil Rights Memorial, designed by the Vietnam Memorial architect Maya Lin, powerfully depicts forty lives lost in the civil rights struggle. In my travels throughout the South, my sympathy toward black Americans and what they as a group endured from their countrymen grew by the day. It was disturbing to me that segregation was an accepted practice in many parts of our country well within my lifetime, and even that of my children despite the emancipation act signed into law over 100 years ago.

My next stop was Selma, fifty minutes away by auto, but worlds apart from Montgomery otherwise. To the extent Montgomery has come to recognize and memorialize the Civil Rights Movement, Selma appears to be its polar opposite. The town's main street appeared little changed from fifty years ago, with a Rexall Drug Store amid 50s-style buildings and facades in disrepair. Walking about the area, I felt as if I was in the movie *Back to the Future*. The fresh popcorn available in the local drugstore, the corner grocery shop, counter delis and the like all added to the nostalgia.

Fig. 6 - Downtown Selma, AL, with infamous Edmund Pettus Bridge in background

In conversations I initiated with a couple of local, white male retirees, they downplayed the efforts and significance of the civil rights movement in this area and suggested to me that the integration attitudes of the Selma community go back to much earlier times. Selma was where the historic march to Montgomery began in 1965 to support voting rights for blacks. Two marches were stopped by the Alabama State Police, the first in a violent, deadly manner known as the Sunday Massacre. The third and final march did succeed, only because the U.S. Supreme Court ruled these walks were constitutional, and the National Guard was sent to protect the safety of the marchers. Crossing the Alabama River via the Edmund Pettus Bridge at Selma, the marchers walked approximately fifty miles. Starting out with a few hundred participants, it culminated with twenty-five thousand people trudging the final leg of the march to the steps of the State Capitol in Montgomery.

When I feigned ignorance about the march in conversing with a museum volunteer, he voiced his opinion that "it was no big deal" because the marchers were able to sleep on farmlands on route to Montgomery. Seems to me, any way you look at it, it still was a fifty-mile walk.

From Selma I drove four hours north to Huntsville, AL, arriving late evening and looking forward to a tour of the NASA Space Center the following morning. With the Saturn V rocket launchers spiking up from the landscape like skyscrapers, it was impossible to miss the entrance to NASA's Huntsville Space Museum. It showcased the history of space travel from its earliest beginning to the present and included an IMAX movie showing the operation of the International Space Station; I came away with an overwhelming sense of the enormity and complexity of our county's space program.

On a day of clear blue skies and seventy- degree temperatures, I drove to a nearby popular state forest, Montesanto, for an hour's hike, and then to the Huntsville Botanical Gardens. Among the highlights were the varied and exquisite plant and tree specimens throughout park-like grounds and a separate area with a model train operating in a thousand-square-foot forest of bonsai plantings, which were in scale with the train to create a miniature-forested countryside.

My route toward Tupelo, MS, passed a natural stone formation in western Alabama known as the Natural Bridge. I stopped for a brief walk to this formation, considered the longest such structure east of the Continental Divide. Entering Tupelo, I was surprised by the extensive array of motels along Highway 45 and thought their number reflected the needs of tourists visiting this birthplace of Elvis Presley. Instead, I was informed that Tupelo is a center for the wholesale furniture trade and twice a year exhibitions attract buyers from all over the world. Driving through the showplace area the next morning, I saw acres of buildings that housed both permanent and temporary furniture collections of all the major manufacturers.

A short ride into Tupelo took me to the tiny house where Elvis Presley in 1935 was born along with his twin brother who died at birth. Never having been an Elvis fan, my time here was short, but I did enjoy reading letters about his youth written by his friends and acquaintances. Of particular interest was one from a store clerk who told the story of Elvis as a young teen coming into his store with his mother to buy a .22 caliber rifle. Mrs. Presley discussed the gun's dangers with Elvis and then forbade him from buying it as well as a bicycle, which she felt could also cause him injury. According to the letter, Elvis was visibly upset and the clerk, in an effort to placate him, suggested he buy a guitar. Elvis balked at the idea, but when he realized his mother was adamant about not giving in to him, he reluctantly agreed to have her buy the guitar. And, as they say, "the rest is history"!

Fig. 7 - Elvis Presley's two-room house in Tupelo, MS, where he was born on January 8, 1935

Tupelo is an entry point on the Natchez Trace, a 444-mile-long scenic parkway administered by the National Park Service. It follows the Natchez Trace, an old Indian path that became the major overland route between the Gulf Coast and upper Mississippi and Ohio River Valleys. It stretches from Nashville across the Tennessee Valley, through the Shoals of Alabama to Nachez, overlooking the Mississippi River. In the 18th and 19th centuries the sparsely-settled territory was dominated by wild animals and bandits and the Trace was known as "Devil's Backbone." Despite the dangers, it was a popular travel route in those times, finally becoming obsolete after the introduction of steamboats in the 1820s. It was at an inn along this route that, by most accounts, explorer extraordinaire Meriwether Lewis committed suicide in 1809.

Paying heed to the strictly enforced speed limit of 50 mph, I patiently steered my way south, as the road passed quiet woodlands and extensive marshland and waterways, and it was punctuated only by roadside markers of historically significant sites along its 300-mile route. An interesting turnoff was at Frenchman's Creek, halfway between Tupelo and Jackson, MS, where a log cabin café run by a Christian school offered a hearty, delicious, and inexpensive lunch.

I motored into Mississippi's capitol city of Jackson in late afternoon. As was the case in Montgomery, the downtown thoroughfares were light with both vehicle and pedestrian traffic. I checked into the *Capitol Inn*, a midtown hotel close to the State Capitol and several antebellum buildings that were occupied by Union forces and thus spared destruction. I toured the Old State Capital Building with its well presented historical exhibits. That evening I dined at an upscale restaurant, *Chars*, in North Jackson. The state legislature was in session, and since Jackson is the state capital, there was the usual inclusion of politicians as well as the inevitable lobbyists, their female cohorts, and a collection of well-dressed professional types. The ambience of the restaurant was "yuppie hip" and the food was excellent.

I left Jackson early the next morning anxious to see Vicksburg and arrived there after lunch. My first stop was the Vicksburg National Military Park and Museum, which I toured from my automobile. The guide I hired to accompany me in my car to describe the sites was an octogenarian school teacher who had suffered a mild stroke the previous year, which restricted her mobility. Charlotte moved to Vicksburg over fifty years ago from Missouri when her chemist husband took a position with an analytical lab in Vicksburg.

To my surprise and delight, this frail former teacher proceeded to out talk me over the next several hours. With unbridled energy she vigorously demonstrated an encyclopedic knowledge of the events that shaped the future of our country: Vicksburg during the Civil War, its fall, and the reopening of the Mississippi River under the control of Union forces. Her enthusiasm was infectious as she told stories of Vicksburg's historic past. An interesting piece of trivia ferreted from this history lesson with Charlotte was that during the Civil War, should a person called to serve demur, he could pay someone three hundred dollars to go off to battle in his place. While this practice was discouraged in the South, it was not in the North. One of our former presidents, because he was supporting a family at the time, did pay another person to serve in the Union Army in his place. Thus, Grover Cleveland avoided military service.

My tour of the battlefield included a visit to an original gunboat of the Union Army, sunk by a Confederate mine. The *U.S.S. Cairo* was salvaged in the waters off Vicksburg in 1960, much of it still intact with a myriad of artifacts on board. The boat is now displayed in the adjacent museum. At day's end I checked into the *Cedar Grove Mansion*, once the grandest of the antebellum Vicksburg plantations.

Fig. 8 - Park Guide Charlotte aside salvaged Union Army gunboat, U.S.S. Cairo, Vicksburg National Military Park, MS

After breakfast the following morning, a tour was given of *Cedar Grove*, which served as a Union military hospital during the Civil War and housed the Confederate President Jefferson Davis during his postwar imprisonment. General Ulysses S. Grant lived there during the Union's occupation of Vicksburg and those same rooms are available for rent by guests today.

On my walking tour of downtown Vicksburg I stopped at a small candy store under the name *Bierdenharn Museum of Coca Cola Memorabilia*. It was there in 1894 that the proprietor, Joseph Biedenharn, first bottled *Coca Cola* for sale as a carbonated drink. Previously, cola was available only as a regional soda fountain drink.

I also toured the Vicksburg County Museum, which preserves extensive memorabilia from the pre- through post-Civil War period. A Civil War buff could easily spend a full day there absorbing and reflecting on the events of that time so thoroughly portrayed in its many rooms.

Lunch was a delightful experience at a local café overlooking the Mississippi River, where I enjoyed a delicious "poh boy" oyster sandwich. The lightly breaded and fried oysters, fresh and juicy, became my fast food indulgence throughout my southern swing. I was reticent to leave the charm and history of Vicksburg behind, yet I wanted to visit a couple of sites along the Natchez Trace and reach Natchez before darkness fell.

The fifty-seven day siege of Vicksburg culminated in a Union victory on July 4, 1863. Because of the uncompromised loyalty of its citizenry to the Confederate cause during that time, what followed was considered by some to be a brutal and repressive occupation by Union forces. For some 80 years thereafter Vicksburg would not acknowledge our country's July 4th Independence Day.

Today, with the introduction of legalized gambling in casinos located on Indian land or a body of water, Vicksburg is firmly enmeshed in the 21st century. I visited two of these riverboats, observed the patrons, and concluded most of them appear to occupy the lowest rung of the economic ladder. Not surprisingly, the adjacent neighborhood is dotted with signs: "Pawn Shop," Title Mortgages," and "Loans," attached to drab, corrugated buildings, which tell a sad story of the plight of many of the casino's customers. An unfortunate incident was shared with me by a waitress at the *Cedar Grove Inn*. She recounted the experience of someone she knew who was told by her husband that he had just lost his money, family car, and home. Shortly thereafter he hung himself! Tragically, I believe similar stories can be found in many casino towns throughout America.

I arrived in Natchez as darkness fell, expecting that it would be easy to find a room, since I was told at the Visitor's Center there would be no problem this time of year. Apparently someone forgot to tell the volunteers at the Visitor's Center that a conference of 1,000 Episcopalians was in town, so finding a room would be a challenge. I ended up at a downtown hotel, the *Eola Inn*, which was also the headquarters of the Episcopalian group. That evening I drove to the outskirts of Natchez to a restaurant in one of the areas of several antebellum mansions. The atmosphere was charming and the highlight of the meal was the appetizer, fried green tomatoes….wow! Firm, green tomatoes dipped in milk, flour, and eggs, covered with bread crumbs and skillet-fried until brown. What a treat!

Before the Civil War, Natchez had the most millionaires per capita in the U.S., and it shows with over 500 antebellum structures inside the city limits. After church the following morning, I toured several home sites in and around Natchez, each with its individual character. Driving about the perimeter of Natchez near the old city cemetery, I noted a familiar but strangely placed object: an operating oil well pumping away in the backyard of a modest home site. In the early 1900s oil replaced cotton as the economic engine for Natchez and its surroundings, and some of these individual wells are still producing.

Fig. 9 - Operating oil well in backyard of private home, Natchez, MS

I continued to the town of St. Francisville, an 18th-century settlement just over the border into Louisiana and home for a time to the naturalist and bird illustrator John James Audubon. The *St. Francisville Inn*, a restored Victorian mansion turned B&B in the village center, was an ideal place to overnight. Unfortunately, heavy rains on the last day of January curtailed my morning walk; instead I visited two popular plantations of which the first was *Oakley House*. Its owner had hired J.J. Audubon as a resident tutor for his child, during which time Audubon completed over 40 of his final illustrations. Additionally, his wife Lucy tutored local women to help pay for the publication of his work.

The highlight of my visit to *Oakley House* did not center around Audubon but rather the plantation grounds and museum that chronicled slave life on the plantation. The original slave quarters were open for inspection, and the museum included comprehensive accounts from a variety of sources of what life as a slave was like not only during a typical 24 hours but during a lifetime of bondage.

Having concluded my visit to *Oakley House*, I next toured the *Greenwood Plantation*, built by William Ruffin Barrow in 1830 and considered the South's finest example of classic colonial architecture. With twenty-eight columns surrounding the Greek revival style house, it was a magnificent sight. Greenwood was open to visitors for limited tours and there is a separate bed and breakfast inn on the grounds.

I arrived at the plantation on a rainy, dreary morning and it appeared deserted. While I was standing on the front porch waiting for the building to open, a portly gentleman appeared outside and enthusiastically greeted me. I responded to his hospitable demeanor saying I was interested in touring the mansion. He said the tour guide was off on Mondays, so he would take me around. To my surprise and delight, Richard's family has been living in the area for six generations, and as the owner of Greenwood, he has resided there for the past thirty-seven years, currently with his wife and children. His personally-escorted tour included an hour orientation in his living room where Richard recounted the history of the area and the plantation, as well as his family history. Following our conversation, I was shown most of the other rooms of the grand residence. *Greenwood Plantation* has been a popular setting for motion pictures and continues to attract filmmakers to its majestic structure set among moss-draped live oak trees and reflecting ponds. The miniseries *North and South* was filmed at Greenwood and the plantation also provided temporary living quarters for Halle Berry, Billy Bob Thornton, and other cast members of the Oscar-winning film, *Monster's Ball*.

I made a brief stop at Port Hudson, which was the site of the longest battle of the Civil War by twenty-four hours: fifty-eight versus Vicksburg's fifty-seven days. Since it was fought concurrently with the Vicksburg siege, the battle for the lesser known Port Hudson was consigned to relative obscurity. Arriving that evening outside of Baton Rouge, Louisiana's capital city, and with a second day of heavy rain, I decided to forego a tour of downtown Baton Rouge, which seemed to offer little other than two State Capitol Buildings. One was the original fortress-like structure along the rivers that served as the first state capitol, while the second, the tallest State Capitol Building in the U.S., thirty-four stories, remains a testament to Louisiana's legendary governor, Hughie Long.

Alternatively, I drove fifty miles west to Lafayette, the "Capital of Cajun Country," to begin a three day sojourn through the bayous on my way to Mardi Gras weekend in New Orleans. I toured an old sugar plantation in St. Marysville, the structure of which was different from others I had seen. Its design is referred to as "raised Creole cottage," comparable to the 20th-century raised ranches common in the States.

Lafayette is the cultural and commercial center of Cajun country and the ideal starting point for exploring French-speaking Louisiana. The Jean Lafitte Cultural Center offered an outstanding video presentation covering the history of the Acadian people (Cajuns), as well as a museum depicting events and displaying artifacts pertaining to Acadian history. From the time of their arrival after deportation from Nova Scotia, they managed to survive and even prosper in spite of dire circumstances. While in Lafayette, I visited the St. John's Evangelist Cathedral whose courtyard housed a huge 450-year-old live oak tree considered the second largest of its species in the U.S.A. with an 8 ft. diameter trunk and 215 ft. diameter canopy. My lunch was at *PreJeans Restaurant*, a semi-haute tribute to southern Louisiana's holy trinity of salt, fat, and deep frying. My selection of fried oysters and crab fish bisque validated its well deserved reputation for superb cuisine.

Fig. 10 – Live oak (450 years old) with 215-ft. canopy and 8-ft. diameter trunk on grounds of St. Johns Evangelist Cathedral, Lafayette, LA

I departed Lafayette via Breaux Bridge, the "Crawfish Capital of the World," to the historic town of St. Martinsville, an early 1700s military post that was later a settling place for displaced Acadians, who were driven from Nova Scotia by the English. St. Martinsville is home to the Evangeline oak, the ancient moss-covered tree said to be where Evangeline met her long lost fiancée, the story of which is the focus of Longfellow's famous poem.

Further south along the Cajun route was New Iberia, where I spent the evening. The following morning I toured *Shadows-on-the-Teche*, an 1834 plantation. It is an exquisite site once described by noted filmmaker Elia Kazan as "the most beautiful house I have seen in the South."

Nearby was Avery Island, home of the McIllhenny Company, maker of the world's best known and widely-consumed tabasco sauce. This company has created a monopoly with a product consisting of little more than pepper, salt, and vinegar....go figure!

That afternoon I departed from the small port town of Patterson, twenty miles up river into the Bayou, with native Captain Cajun Jack on his motor boat. It was cold, windy, and raw and we had to pass through the locks of a dam to get into the swampland. Despite the uncomfortable weather, the trip was stimulating, as I had the opportunity to see the floating homes of the few remaining Cajun families living in the Bayou. According to Cajun Jack, there are only about fifty people still living in the Bayous, and they profit well from their crawfish and catfish hauls. One would never know the economic benefits are as significant as they are when viewing the ramshackle appearance of their houseboats.

Fig. 11 - Cajun "mobile home" on Louisiana bayous

I arrived later that evening in the bustling town of Houma, where despite a seemingly endless stream of motels along the commercial strip, I was unable to find a room. Since Houma was not a tourist attraction, I was perplexed as to why all these motels should be filled to capacity. As it turned out, the proximity of Houma to the offshore oil/gas drilling platforms make it the departure point for workers being transported by helicopter to and from these rigs. High winds during the day had grounded the helicopters, and the workers were forced to remain behind, thus taxing the capacity of Houma's motels. I located a bed & breakfast inn run by a native Cajun couple, Leland and Sally Crochet, who were wonderful hosts for my two-night stay in their home.

Both are direct descendants of the original Cajuns (French speaking Catholic Acadians) who were exiled from Canada when the English took over in 1755. Put to sea in overcrowded and poorly equipped ships, the Acadians were refused entry by the American colonies on the East Coast and had to make their way to French Louisiana. Others who had been imprisoned in England were eventually given land grants by Spain and returned to that same region of southeastern U.S. To this day, these resilient, independent people have retained their culturally distinct identity.

The Cajun story is a tragic account of cruelty endured at the hands of the governing English during that period. A riveting portrayal of that experience is recounted in the Crochet family genealogy by a recently deceased ancestor of Sally and Leland, Dr. Verne Pitre. *Poor Woman Revisited* tells the story of his maternal great-great-great-great grandparents and their experiences during that tumultuous period of their lives. It is reprinted in its entirety herewith:

POOR WOMAN REVISITED
By Dr Verne Pitre

I can only try to imagine the anguish of my maternal great-great-great-great grandparents, Yves and Pelagie Benoist(1) Crochet, as they were herded aboard ship by the English in 1759 for deportation from Acadie(2).

Like other Acadians who would not flee in fear to the French territory of New Brunswick, they had incurred the wrath of Governor Charles Lawrence. A moody, rash tyrant, Lawrence had worked out schemes to expel the Acadians whether or not they accepted his condition of swearing allegiance to the British crown in order to remain there

Yves(3) was born September 1, 1732 in Megrit, Cotes-du-Nord, France. He migrated to Louisbourg, Isle Royale before 1758. Pelagie(4), was born in 1741 in Pisiguit, Acadie. She lived there, also the birthplace of her father, until the Benoist family fled in 1752 to escape the English and re-settled at L'Anse-an-Matelot, Isle St. Jean. Pelagie and Yves were married February 6, 1758--less than six months before the fortress of Louisbourg, where they had taken refuge, fell to English troops on July 26(5).

After the capitulation of Louisbourg, Yves and his 18-year-old wife were deported to France, accompanied by Pelagie's two brothers, Gregoire 15 and Daniel 10, and two sisters, Anne 13 and Marguerite 8. Since nothing is known of the whereabouts of Pelagie's parents at that time, it is likely they died before the deportation and her orphaned brothers and sisters were already in her care.

It had to be heart-tearing for a newly-wed at age 18 to be persecuted, stripped of her possessions, forcibly removed from a land she had helped to colonize, and have thrust upon her the total responsibility for four siblings, ages 8-15.

The deportees arrived in Rochefort, France October 1, 1759. Despite their sad plight, they were more fortunate than the hundreds of other Acadians who were lost at sea after being forced aboard less-than-seaworthy vessels or the thousands more who were shuttled repeatedly from Maine to the West Indies as undesirables. From Rochefort they went to St. Malo and resided in the parishes of Megrit and St. Servan

Pelagie and Yves became parents to nine children: sons Jean Guillaume (1760), Francois Louis (1761), Jean Joseph (1763), Yves Jean (1767), Julien (1770), Jean Marin (1774), and daughters Francoise Pelagie (1764), Marguerite Perinne (1766), and Pelagie (1772). Two of the children, Francois Louis and Jean Joseph, died in infancy or very early childhood. Yves, the father, died November 23, 1773 and was buried at Megrit, Cotes-du-Nord.

Left at her husband's death with an unborn child and six others in age 1-13, she was yet to suffer the agony and endure the death of her namesake and two-year-old daughter, Pelagie, in 1774. The death occurred just 28 days after the birth of Jean Marin. The boy himself must have become an early tragedy since he was not in the company of his mother and brothers and sisters when, a year later, they began their migration to Louisiana Territory.

Other than the promise of a Spanish land grant, what prompted the widow

Crochet's decision to leave France for Louisiana Territory I have not determined. Undoubtedly the reason must have been serious enough to warrant great patience. She and the surviving five of her children: Jean Guillaume, Francois Pelagie, Marguerite Perinne, Yves Jean, and Julien left Chatellerault for Nantes November 15, 1775. It was nearly ten years--August 12, 1785--before the group was able to sail from Nantes(6) and arrive in New Orleans November 7. (At least one account identifies daughter Marguerite as Pelagie's sister, but that obviously is an error. Marguerite the sister was 8 in 1759 when deported to France and would have been 34 in 1785. Marguerite the daugther, apparently named for Pelagie's sister, was 19 in 1785 and she, not her aunt, made the trip to Louisiana.)

By royal order of the Spanish king in 1783, Acadian migrants had been assured good lands, houses, tools, and subsides until they became self supporting and able to repay the monies expended in their behalf. Since so many Acadians were thrifty and good carpenters, it was determined that they should build their own houses. For this, they were paid a subsidy of $100 per house. Any savings realized in building could be used to purchase cattle for their land. An additional subsidy of two and one-half cents per day per individual for food and clothing was paid, but this proved inadequate and was increased to seven and a half cents. The subsidies continued until 1789.

The land grant Pelagie received was registered in the name of her youngest son, Julien(7), by then at least 15. It was located on the east side of Bayou Lafourche (now Louisiana highway 308) at Thibodaux, about a block north of the street known today as Coulon Road. Another description places the property as 12 arpents(8) above St. Patrick Highway--about the same location. Like other grants, it was six arpents (approximately 1152 feet) in width fronting on the bayou and 40 arpents (approximately 7,680 feet) in depth. Since women were not prohibited from receiving land grants in their own names, it is interesting to speculate why Julien and not Pelagie was registered as owner. Perhaps Pelagie saw her four older children as having attained a measure of security and desired the same for her youngest.

According to the census of January 1, 1789, the tract was bordered on the north by that of Pelagie's daughter and son-in-law, Leonardo and Francoise Crochet de LaGarde(9), and on the south by that of another daughter and son-in-law Joseph and Marguerite Crochet Adam(10). Obviously Spanish authorities made a point of keeping families together.

Julien's ownership of the grant through inhabitation and cultivation for more than 10 years was confirmed December 20, 1803(11). Sometime before, the adjoining property above--that of his sister, Francoise--had been disposed of. Since she was listed as a widow with four sons in the census of January 1, 1791, it is safe to assume that Francoise's husband had died in 1789 or 1790. By 1792, she had remarried.

Patent 213, which confirmed Julien's ownership of what I regarded as Pelagie's grant, states, "Julien Crochet claims a tract of land, situate (sic) on the left bank of the bayou La Fourche, in the county of La Fourche, containing one hundred and nine and eighty-five hundreds superficial acres, and bounded onthe upper side by lands of Victor Coulon and Peter Aubart, and on the lower by land of Marguerite Crochet. It appears that the claimant did actually inhabit and cultivate the land now claimed on the 20th of December, 1803, and for more than ten consecutive years prior thereto. "Confirmed". The LaGarde, Crochet, and Adam grants are today part of Coulon Plantation.

My line of ancestry comes through the second marriage of Francoise. According to Baton Rouge Diocese Archive records (Vol. 2, p. 207), Francoise married at Plattenville on June 19, 1792 Phillippe Bruze(12), born in Genoa, Italy in 1771. Of this marriage were born daughter Marceline (1800) and son Jean Isadore (1801).

It is believed that the couple resided for a time in New Orleans, moving back to Bayou Lafourche before 1807. In his family tradition, Phillippe was a flat-boat hauler (floating merchant) alond the bayou. A partial land sale to one Claude Francois Giroir, dated October 22, 1810, suggests that they owned a sizeable tract on the right descending bank approximately one and a half miles below the present Lafourche Crossing.

Although the marriage lasted until Phillippe died May 15, 1826 at age 55, it must have been a union of turmoil. There are reports that during a drunken spree Phillippe burned a trunk full of Francoise's family papers, thereby destroying important information. Francoise died February 25, 1836 at age 73 and is buried in old St Joseph Cemetery in Thibodaux.

Jean Isadore Bruce first married Marie LeBlanc in 1825, then Marie Antoinette Richoux(13) on August 30, 1828. One of the offsprings from the later marriage was Joachim Jean Bruce, born April 9, 1835 at Cote Blanche in Lafourche Parish, some 45 miles south of Thibodaux.

Joachim married Pauline Remont(14) August 30, 1860 and they resided at Cut Off, near her parents. One of the children born to them was Marie Annelie Bruce, my maternal grandmother and the principal figure in my book, "Grandma was a Sailmaker: Tales of the Cajun Wetlands", published in 1991 by Blue Heron Press, Thibodaux, La.

In 1901, grandmother became the second wife of Melfort Francois Garpard(15) of Cote Blanche and mother to his children. To them was born one child, Blanche Bernadette, later to be the wife of Ignace Joseph Pitre(16) of Golden Meadow and my mother

Great-great-great-great grandmother Pelagie died at age 83 in Thibodaux at the home of Similien Adam(17). Although no grave marker exists, church records show she was buried in old St. Joseph Cemetery. Page 14 of the "Civil Register of Deaths, Lafourche Interior Parish, La." states "Pelagie Benoit died in Lafourche Interior Parish on 7 May 1824, widow of Ives Crochet, a poor woman."

In 1989 Audrey B. Westerman published some background information on Pelagie in an article entitled, "Pelagie Benoit, A Poor Woman", and Kenneth Toups provided the inventory and public auction records of her estate in two articles appearing in the same publication(18).

At the request of Similien Adam, Pelagie's estate was inventoried and appraised April 16, 1825, then sold at publice auction exactly one month later. Her possessions, their appraised values, and the sale prices(19) were listed as:

1. One feather bed, one straw mattress, one pillow, one sheet, one blanket, and one mosquito-bar, estimated together at $6.00; auctioned for $18.25.

2. One pair of ropes and a small basket, estimated at 75 cents; auction for $1.00

3. One basket, two old shirts, one pair of shoes, and several other rags, estimated at 75 cents; auctioned for 87 1/2 cents.

4. One dress, one shirt, one bath-robe, one pair of stockings, estimated at $1.00; auctioned for $1.31 1/4 cents.

5. One old shirt, eight hankerchiefs (good and bad), estimated $1.00; auctioned for $2.00.

6. One box, knitting needles, one pair of stockings, one shawl, and a roll of brass wire (may have been a circular knitting needle made of brass and used to knit stockings), estimated at $1.00; auctioned for $2.43 3/4.

7. One small pot, one chamber pot, five plates and one coffee box, estimated at 37 1/2 cents; auctioned for 87 1/2 cents.

8. One skirt, one shirt, one bath-robe, and one old blanket, estimated at $1.50; auctioned for 25 cents.

> Total appraised value......................$12.37 1/2
>
> Total auction revenue......................$27.00

All of the money possessed by Pelagie at her death amounted to one dollar and one bit of "escalin" ($1.12 1/2). It is recorded on the inventory that this sum was paid out. Presumably, it went to Joseph Lambert and Mathurin Ayo for the appraisal

The auction revenue of $27.00 was applied to other debts. Due Similian Adam for care and board during Pelagie's last illness was $14.00. Pierre Schwab, the auctioneer, charged $1.00 for his services; 75 cents was spent for "rum for the auction"; Andre Adam(20) claimed $2.50 as payment "for 5 planks which served to make a coffin". The balance of $8.75 is unaccounted for and I suppose that to have been applied to expenses incurred by the court of Judge Pierre Daspit for the proceedings. Poor Woman!

(1) Later spelled "Benoit"

(2) Now "Nova Scotia"

(3) Son of Guillaume and Julienne Durand Crochet

(4) Daughter of Claude and Elizabeth Therriot Benoist

(5) Their marriage on records in the Archives Nationales in France

(6) Aboard the ship "L'Amite", as the French knew it, or "L'Amistad", as the Spanish called the same vessel; not aboard two separate vessels bearing those names, as some confused researches have stated.

(7) The older sons are married. Jean Guillaume (recorded as "Juan" by Spanish civil authorities) wed Maria Boudreaux in New Orleans in 1785 and is believed to have been living there; Yves Jean claimed a land grant of his own, confirmed in 1803 and shown as tract 8, section 165 on an 1858 map of the Southeast District of Louisiana

(8) an arpent is a French measurement of approximately 192 linear feet or 5/6

of an acre.

(9) Later spelled with "de" as a prefix.

(10) According to St. Louis Cathedral records, Marguerite and Francoise were wed in New Orleans on the same day, November 24, 1785.

(11) "American State Papers", volume 2, page 412

(12) Later spelled "Bruce"

(13) Daughter of Pierre and Felicite Duhe Richoux

(14) Daughter of Joseph and Pauline Lee Remont

(15) Son of Leon and Pamela Lefort Gaspard

(16) Son of Maxmillien and Leocade Dantin Pitre

(17) Believed to be the grandson (son of daughter Marguerite) recorded at birth as "Similano"

(18) "Terrebonne Life Lines", Terrebonne Genealogical Society, Vol. 8, No. 3, Fall 1989.

(19) "Inventory & Verbal Process of Sale Estate Left by the Deceased Pelagie Benoit, Widow of Ives Crochet, 16 April 1825 and 16 May 1825," recorded in Lafourche Parish Courthouse

(20) An older grandson and brother of Similien

During one of my many conversations with Leland, he encouraged me to drive seventy miles to the lower bayou and hamlet of Cocodrie. The road paralleled the bayous, and shrimp boats were visible at the backyard docks of many homes along the route. I learned something curious about the role of these boats in the local economy when I stopped to speak with a man I saw attending to his boat. He told me he and his kind were self employed, owned their boats, and trolled for shrimp; their fortunes (as with most fishermen) was dependent on the weather, regulations, experience, and plain luck!

As I neared the end of the road, I saw numerous cabins built on stilts which served as seasonal camps for the hunting/fishing enthusiasts. My drive terminated at the *Cocodrie Inn*, a popular tourist hotel on the water's edge that was deserted this time of year. Nearby I visited the Marine Research Lab, housed in a large contemporary structure and operated under the auspices of Louisiana State University. The extensive building complex was constructed in marshland twenty-five years ago and is sinking at an alarming rate. This suggests a limited future for the complex and it appears that nothing can be done to save it. In the past this facility had been frequented and utilized by famed oceanographer Jacques Cousteau.

Tragically, since my visit, Hurricanes Katrina and Rita ravaged the entire Gulf Coast in August/September, 2005. Plummeted by high winds, heavy rain, and storm surges that breached the levies of New Orleans, the region suffered catastrophic loss of lives and property, the extent of which was still being assessed a year later. In 2006 I called Leland Crochet to inquire about the hurricane damage to their vicinity of Louisiana. To my surprise, he said the main damage was from the flooding due to Rita, and after the waters receded, only modest damage was visible. The Inn, Marine Research Lab, and private homes and camps were intact.

On my last evening in Houma, I visited the Water Life Museum, where a local Cajun band played and sang the songs of their culture. It was a boisterous and festive atmosphere much enjoyed by both the audience and the band members; it was a fitting climax to my visit to the area.

I left Houma before sunrise for the one-hour drive to New Orleans, where I arrived at the elegant *Windsor Court Hotel*, an establishment with all the luxury and charm of the finest European hotels, adjacent to the French Quarter. Fortunately my suite was available for early check-in, after which I was off for a walk to explore the central part of the city. Not only was this my first visit to New Orleans, it was Mardi Gras Weekend and the festiveness of the occasion was evident all around.

The D-Day Museum was within walking distance (couple of miles) from my hotel, and I took the opportunity to visit it. In truth, my interest in WW II, especially the Pacific theater, dates back to when, as an eight-to-ten- year old, I crawled about the halls and closets of our apartment outfitted in full army regalia in search of "the enemy"! War movies of the time like *Sands of Iwo Jima, Bataan, Guadalcanal Diary,* and others glorified (at least in my young mind) the exploits of U.S. soldiers and made me want to emulate their heroics. I didn't even need an attacking enemy to carry out my missions. No wonder I was selected class dramatist in my high school graduating class.

The museum's exhibits presented an in-depth and emotionally-moving story of our country's participation in World War II, with emphasis on the D-Day invasion and the war's Pacific theater. Movie documentaries chronicled the events and were powerful reminders of the difficult years our country faced in an all-out effort to defeat the military might of Germany and Japan. Pictorial and narrative portrayals of the many battles the allied forces waged during that time were equally riveting. The display of wartime artifacts and original dialogue of combat troops made for a compelling story of bravery and courage.

For lunch the casual and friendly *Acme Oyster Bar* was *the* place to go for those fresh, plump bivalves. This French Quarter eatery was bustling while a long line of patrons patiently waited outside for their turn to savor the seafood delights within. After I satisfied my taste buds and stomach with a crock of Cajon fish chowder and a slew of raw oysters, I set out for a walk along the streets of the French Quarter, including the renowned Bourbon Street. What a party! And at 2:00 in the afternoon! People were all over the place: on balconies, sidewalks, the street, and the bars…all those bars! From middle-aged businessmen in their blue suits to scantily clad females of all ages and persuasions, the revelry seemed to go unabated. It was difficult to imagine what the nighttime hours would hold.

It seemed to me the threads that weave this fabric of fun together for Mardi Gras (no doubt assisted by copious quantities of alcoholic beverages) were the beads of various sizes, shapes, and colors that everybody was intent on collecting. Females, especially, displayed their wares with otherwise benign behavior to entice one to give their beads away. Normally private body parts were not a rarity to be seen among the throngs of revelers!

At day's end I relaxed in the spacious, elegant lobby of the *Windsor Court*, awaiting my friend Cheryl's arrival from Connecticut. I had met her the past year and we came to enjoy each other's company and shared many pleasant times together. With her infectious smile and hearty laugh, she is a very attractive lady who is a delight to be around. I was looking forward to spending time with her. Despite the late evening crowds and traffic, Cheryl's airport taxi arrived on schedule and we enjoyed a late dinner at a quaint restaurant in the French Quarter, followed by our first walk through wild and raucous Bourbon Street. I should not say "walk" because it is impossible to walk; one kind of oozes one's way through the packed crowds in glacial fashion.

Saturday, the 5th of February, brought forth a delightful day of sunshine and warm temperatures, ideal for a walk about the central area of Mardi Gras-crazed New Orleans. We strolled along the riverfront, Jackson Square, and Royal Street where the pricey art galleries and antique stores are located. Later in the day we watched a couple of parades before returning to our hotel for an exquisite dinner in the Grill Room. After a clothing change, we returned to the streets of the French Quarter to watch the major parades of Mardi Gras. We could take just so much of the congestion and craziness, and we eventually retreated to the opposite end of the French Quarter to listen to a jazz performance in less crowded surroundings.

Fig. 12 - Author and friend Cheryl, overlooking Jackson Square during Mardi Gras weekend in New Orleans, LA

During the evening extravaganza while we were in the most packed area of the quarter, I had my pocket relieved of loose cash. Fortunately the amount taken was modest, and although I lamented the loss of the money, I felt it was a relatively inexpensive lesson and reminder to me to never, ever, let my guard down on security issues. Our evening ended with a nightcap in the hotel bar where revelers abounded well into the night.

The following Sunday morning Cheryl and I were hoping to see more of New Orleans, especially the Garden district, but unfortunately all the parade routes were scheduled to be closed by noon, which would give us limited time to see the sites, return to our hotel, and be out of the area by noon on our way to the airport. We decided to leave the city early and spend our remaining time in the vicinity of the airport so she could be assured of catching her scheduled flight home; it also afforded us time to take in a movie and have lunch.

From the airport I continued my drive toward Baton Rouge where I found lodging outside the city and settled in for a good nights rest after watching the Super Bowl. Reflecting on the events of those few days, I've tried to understand the ingredients of the party mix that takes place during Mardi Gras. I witnessed and sensed the friendly, carefree attitudes despite the excess alcohol consumption. Maybe it was the swarm of policemen and security helicopters hovering above that discouraged, for the most part, the kinds of activities which can occur in crowds of this size. I am sure there were incidents, but overall the theme was about having fun (not withstanding my stolen cash); I believe this was due to the constant bead exchanging, which was the prevailing form of communication between the people. These necklaces are tossed to the hand-waving crowds from balconies, parade floats, and just about anywhere. For those more sedate participants, an almost unlimited variety of the beads may be purchased in the stores. In summary, our New Orleans at Mardi Gras was a unique experience to be treasured but not necessarily repeated.

I left Baton Rouge for Galveston the following morning with a fever. It was the first time on my trip that I was feeling less than 100 per cent. Arriving in Galveston by late afternoon, I visited the Moody Garden Recreational Complex. This modern facility consisted of three huge pyramidal structures, one housing a rain forest, the second an aquarium exhibit, and the third an IMAX theater. With an adjacent hotel and convention center, Moody's is geared to be a destination resort for both the business and recreational traveler.

I found a nearby motel and retired early, hoping for a good night's sleep. Unfortunately my mood was somber; earlier that evening I had received a message that the daughter of a very good friend of mine was tragically killed in a snowmobile accident in upper New York state while on holiday. Through no fault of hers, this bright, beautiful twenty-year-old college student, from a close and loving family, will never realize her ambitions. Being a father and grandfather, I could appreciate, but not fully comprehend, the intolerable pain in that family right now. Such tragedies provide an ongoing reminder of the fragility of life and I wished at the moment I was home with my family.

After a restless night's sleep, fever and all, I took an early morning walk though the historic section of Galveston, followed by a tour of the *Ocean Star*, a decommissioned oil drilling rig previously in service in the Gulf of Mexico and now stationed in the shallow waters off the docks. The self- guided tour offered fascinating insights into the technology of drilling for oil and gas in the seabed off the Gulf Coast. Current drilling technology has enabled companies to drill over seven miles deep into the ocean floor! A class of petroleum engineering students from nearby Texas A&M University was led on a tour by their professor, a former platform driller. I remained within earshot of his lectures, which provided detailed descriptions of the rig's operation. I especially appreciated hearing these descriptions since my former company supplied industrial diamonds and related products to the drilling companies.

It was a short walk to the Galveston museum, which highlighted the hurricane in September, 1900, considered the greatest natural disaster in our country's history (at least as measured by the over six thousand lives lost). I had previously read *Isaac's Storm*, a true account of that historic catastrophe and the National Weather Service person, Isaac Klein, the book tells of his futile efforts at the time to get anyone to believe him that this killer storm was going to be upon them very soon. He himself lost his wife during the hurricane's landfall and his remaining life was dramatically influenced by those events.

The museum's program included a well-documented movie and narrative that traced the sequence and aftermath of the storm. Another section was devoted to the exploits of the infamous pirate Jean Lafitte, who spent three- and one-half years in the early 1820s enjoying the fruits of his plunders on the island of Galveston. He was finally asked by the U.S. Navy to leave the U.S., which he did, meeting his demise not long thereafter. A movie chronicles his life and times in entertaining fashion.

After lunch I drove 200 miles south to Padre Island off the coast of Corpus Christi. I arrived after dark and checked into a motel at the north end of this barrier island. Much of Padre Island, including South Padre Island, is a national park refuge; the remaining parts are a burgeoning area of commerce abounding with upscale residences, restaurants, and other supporting infrastructure. The area seems to be the current real estate "hot spot"! Further south toward the Mexican border, South Padre Island caters to the spring-break crowd where some 200,000 college students descend on the beaches. Drinking is legal on the beaches and round-the-clock revelry the order of the day and night!

My fever subsided, but with the heavy fog from the night before still present, it didn't make any sense to follow the beach route further south. I went instead to Corpus Christi, where I toured the U.S.S. Lexington, a World War II aircraft carrier damaged numerous times during the war. The ship is moored dockside adjacent to the Texas State Aquarium, which has a collection of various fish and marine animals comparable to other aquariums with seemingly nothing in particular to distinguish it from most such marine attractions

It was a two-hour drive northwest to San Antonio, where my first task was to make reservations for an upcoming visit by my daughter and four grandchildren who would be here during the February school vacation. I planned to fly home for several days and then return with them to spend a week in San Antonio before continuing on with my journey.

Finding a suitable hotel with available rooms along the San Antonio River Walk for that period was a problem because a convention of 6,000 school administrators was being held in the city that same week. I wanted a hotel along the River Walk for the convenience and experience of staying in downtown San Antonio. After a few unsuccessful inquiries, I came upon the *Drury Inn and Suite Hotel* located on the River Walk. With some creative juggling of room selections and the friendly cooperation of the hotel's front desk clerk, I was able to procure the necessary reservations for all of us the following week. The hotel was accessible by foot to all the popular attractions of San Antonio and the rooms were on the same level as the swimming pool, which would make for an enjoyable week for all of us.

Having taken care of that important issue, I managed an afternoon boat ride on the adjacent San Antonio River and followed that with a late dinner at the immensely popular *Boudreau's* on the River Walk. The house specialty, blackened prime rib, was extraordinary: uniquely prepared, tasty, tender and generous. With several other steak and rib selections on their menu, *Boudreau's* would be a top choice for my beef-loving grandchildren and I reserved a table along the River Walk for the last evening of our holiday.

As the first leg of my adventure came to a close, it was apparent to me that the experience was about more than map points. Much of my joy and satisfaction were framed by the people I met along the way and the rich educational experiences of museums and historical memorials. Traveling through the South, my deepest learning experiences include the tragic realities of our country's Civil War and the plight of blacks during the earliest days of our country's history and even into 20th-century America.

My laptop was a welcome, albeit inconsistent, traveling companion. E-mails to and from family and friends provided a measure of continuity with those back home, as did online reading of local papers, such as *The Hartford Courant* and *The Westerly Sun*. What proved annoying, though, was the inconsistency I found in the various ways of connecting the laptop to the internet. The prestige and location of a particular hotel did not ensure ease of connection. Adjacent to the Huntsville NASA Space Center, arguably one of our country's most technologically advanced sites, was located the Marriott Hotel, which had limited and restricted wireless connections. On the other hand, whenever I stayed at inexpensive chain motels, especially *Comfort Inns*, there were reliable wireless connections throughout the facility that proved to be quite "comforting" for my computing needs.

I assembled my travel inventory in preparation for my flight home, as well as for the next leg of my journey into the Southwest. Mom's 88th birthday was the 11th of February and I would be in Connecticut the following day, and I looked forward to seeing her in her usual convivial mood. After catching up on several personal and business matters, I would return to San Antonio with the "Alamo Amigos Gang" for some fun, camaraderie, and adventure in and around San Antonio.

LEG TWO: SOUTHWEST

After my brief "home" stay and with gratitude to family and friends who provided me with temporary sleeping quarters, this homeless itinerant returned to San Antonio with grandsons Jake (16 yrs.) and Ian (13 yrs,) where we joined my daughter, Cher, and her children, Alyssa (11 yrs.) and Zach (13 yrs.), who had arrived the previous day. Our five days together were wonderful. We toured the hill country northwest of San Antonio, which included a visit to the LBJ Ranch, and Fredericksburg, a charming town of German heritage with what is probably the widest main street of any American town or city. Chester Nimitz, the famous WWII admiral, was born in Fredericksburg, a fact that accounts for the Pacific War Museum located in the downtown area. Its exhibits and collection of war memorabilia rival those of the New Orleans D-Day Museum. We also visited a subterranean cave and took a drive through a wild game reserve, which was the highlight for all of us.

The weather was pleasant and well suited for outdoor activities, and our hotel's location on the River Walk was ideal for walking about central San Antonio. We visited the Alamo and other early Spanish missions, took in a couple of IMAX movies, and enjoyed a scenic boat ride on the river adjoining the River Walk. A multitude of gift shops and restaurants on the River Walk kept our stomach's full and wallets light. Dinner at *Boudreau's* on our last night was superb and the perfect way to end our San Antonio adventure.

Fig. 13 - Author's daughter and grandchildren with Alamo in background, San Antonio, TX

When the family returned home, my spirits sank; I was saddened by their departure and lonely in their absence. The four grandchildren don't get to see much of each other as a quartet back home and it was nice watching them having fun together amid all our activities. Despite the age differences, they really get along well with each other and their mutual affection was clearly evident. I was appreciative that Cher was able to rework her teaching schedule to make our reunion possible.

Resuming my travels, I departed San Antonio west to the Hill Country, along the scenic roads passing through places like Bandera (which bills itself as the cowboy capital of the world) and Uvalde at the juncture of the two longest U.S. routes in this country (90 and 83).

Along my route were vast ranch lands supporting cattle, sheep, and, in some cases, domestic and exotic species, where hunters pay very high prices for the opportunity to track and shoot this "wild" game. As I viewed the open spaces of these "hunting farms" (my term), I wondered how this scenario differed from "shooting fish in a barrel"!

The road continued to Brackettville, where fifty years ago John Wayne's movie production company built a full scale replica of the Alamo along with a replication of early San Antonio for the filming of his 1959 movie, *The Alamo*. Since then, this set has been used to film movies, documentaries, and other projects, the most famous being the TV mini series *Lonesome Dove*. From Brackettville I continued west to the Texas border town of Del Rio to overnight and prepare for several days of camping, hiking, and exploration in the picturesque state and national parks of West Texas.

I left Del Rio early the next morning in misty, cool weather, driving towards Seminole Canyon where I hoped to camp and hike the canyons and see the ancient pictographs left behind by the inhabitants of this region over 4,000 years ago. Doris first described this region to me several years ago after she did a solo camping trip on her own personal voyage of self-discovery across the U.S.A. Seems both of us inherited our mother's travel genes!

On the way I passed through the Amistad National Reservation, a huge reservoir created by the confluence of the Rio Grande, Pekoes, and Devils Rivers; the Amistad dam was constructed and is operated to provide flood control and water resources to the region. Driving along the lengthy dam, I noticed that the Mexican/U.S. border was midway on the dam. As a result, in order to cross it, I had to enter Mexico. On my return from the Mexican side, the conversation with the U.S. border agent was a bit awkward; she was skeptical about my explanation for being there. After thoroughly confusing the agent with my unorthodox itinerary, I got the go-ahead sign.

Continuing west, I came to a border checkpoint even though I was not on the border. The major roads paralleling the border now have security checkpoints because of terrorist, drug trafficking, and illegal immigrant concerns. By midday I arrived at the headquarters of Seminole Canyon State Park and proceeded to a tent site overlooking the canyon. There I pitched my one person, fiberglass, pole-supported, nylon tent. It was my first experience with this tent (borrowed from my sister); thirty frustrating minutes later, in a steady drizzle, my nomadic home was complete. Furnishings were basic and included a sleeping bag, pillow, blanket, flashlight, and portable CD player along with my journal in which I had been judiciously recording my daily activities. Due to the wetness of the steep, rocky path leading to the canyon floor, the guided tour of the canyon's pictographs was canceled. Instead I opted for a three-mile hike along the upper trail to the canyon rim. There were grand vistas all about, while cool temperatures kept the considerable rattlesnake population out of sight. I finished the day at the Visitor Center where there were exhibits depicting the region's history, culture, and geology.

My first night camping in Seminole Canyon was a wet one. It rained all night and I woke up to a steady downpour. The weather report called for all day rain, so I elected to break camp and move west to Big Bend National Park, two hundred miles away. The drive to Big Bend continued past the small towns of Sanderson and Marathon along a scenic border route through a portion of the vast Chihuahua Desert. This most southerly of the North American deserts extends from the Rio Grande Valley of southern New Mexico to an area just north of Mexico City. Within its 200,000 square-mile area is a great diversity of landscapes, elevations, flora, and fauna.

Notably, the rain soon subsided and sunny skies highlighted a landscape of expansive plains with rolling hills in the background and a backdrop of rugged peaks 3,000-5,000 feet high. This is a magnificent part of our country; the vastness of the terrain is overwhelming.

Fig. 14 - Main entry to Big Bend National Park, TX

The wild and diverse region of Big Bend remains remote enough that only those targeting it a destination will share in its rich and varied plant and wildlife. Bird watchers take note; more species of birds (over 400) have been counted here than in any other U.S. national park. I arrived at the eastern section of Big Bend National Park, Rio Grande Village, a camping area where I set up my tent amid spectacular rock formations of limestone and shale in rich hues of red and brown. After a quick lunch of sardines, crackers, and fruit, I departed on a six-mile, round-trip hike to Hot Springs, where the trail traversed the ridges and valleys with breathtaking vistas all around. At one point I stopped on top of one of the hills and sat for an hour, surveying my surroundings and appreciating the beauty and solitude. Under bright, sunny skies, I backtracked and proceeded to another hiking area, a popular site for photographing sunsets.

After returning to camp for supper, I attended a talk on dinosaurs by a park ranger at the camp amphitheater. This region is a hotbed of activity for those seeking dinosaur fossils finds of the Cretaceous Period, which includes the largest dinosaurs that ever roamed the earth. It was a lengthy talk on a chilly evening under the starriest sky I have ever seen in my life. The presentation was interesting and the ranger's extensive knowledge of paleontology was impressive.

The following morning began with the most glorious blue sky one could imagine. I broke camp and drove to Chisos Basin, a park campground set into a basin surrounded by the highest peaks of Big Bend National Park and the Chisos Mountains, the southernmost range in the continental U.S. It was a spectacular twenty-nine mile drive and I seemed to be stopping every thirty seconds to photograph ever more interesting scenery My campsite rested below the 7,000+ foot peaks, and by mid morning I headed out for a hike on the Lost Mine Trail, a moderately strenuous five-mile round-trip with a rewarding panorama from the top, one of the grandest in the park. The area epitomizes the beauty found in the high desert regions of our country.

I had to keep reminding myself not to just look out at all the magnificent scenery, because this is also bear and mountain lion country, where it is wise to pay heed to the path in front as well as the beauty around. When I finally passed somebody coming from the opposite direction, I was comfortable again admiring the landscape. I made it to the top of Lost Mine Trail, elevation 6,900 feet, which makes it higher than Mount Washington in the northeast and, in fact, higher than the tallest mountain east of the Mississippi (Mount Mitchell, in North Carolina's Smoky Mountain region). I met another lone hiker at the top who obligingly took my picture as proof of having reached the top of the trail. Although the photographs reveal the region's attractiveness, they cannot do justice to the three-dimensional panoramic beauty of the landscape.

Fig. 15 - View across the Chisos Mountain Range in Big Bend, TX

Returning to camp after the invigorating, sometimes strenuous, trek, I relaxed at my site, appreciative of the opportunity just to be here enjoying the grandeur of the park. There was a lodge and restaurant at the upper part of the basin where I had my first full meal (a forgettable dry, bland, baked trout dinner) since the last of the "Alamos Amigos" returned home three days ago.

I was up by daybreak with frost across my car's windshield and the outside temperature at 30°F. Under sparkling blue skies, I pulled up stakes and drove to the western section of the park via the Ross Highway. This thirty-one mile road passes some of the park's most striking scenery, with several stops at trail heads along the way for hiking. A 2½-hour hike toward the Mule Ears Viewpoint offered magnificent scenery all around. A short, strenuous climb up the Santa Elena Canyon Overlook concluded my stay in the park. Here, the 1,500-ft. high canyon walls, sculptured by the Rio Grande River, defined the Mexican border. The serenity of the natural, undisturbed views from the overlook provided me a lasting image of Big Bend's inordinate beauty.

I exited the park westward via the El Camino del Rio, which parallels the border, passing through Big Bend Ranch State Park; it is another wonderfully scenic roadway. Along the way I made a brief stop at the frontier resort town of Lajitas, where a $300-per-night *Leading Hotels of the World* resort hotel was located. Civilization has arrived in West Texas!

Turning northward toward Presidio, I reflected on the natural beauty of the Chihuahua Desert. There were times when I felt I had died and gone to the southwestern corner of heaven. This is the way it seemed in many instances, especially with the near perfect weather I'd experienced during my Big Bend visit.

It is March 1st and I checked into a roadside motel outside Presidio. A long and refreshing bath and shower (my first in four days) was followed by a Mexican style dinner at a local restaurant and the first restful night's sleep after successive evenings in my nylon bachelor pad. By next morning I was off to Fort Davis, Texas. It was here in 1854 that an army fort, named in honor of then Secretary of War Jefferson Davis, was established to protect westward-bound pioneers from Indian raids. It was the first military post along the San Antonio-El Paso Road and later became a home to the famed African-American buffalo soldiers. The highlight of the day (and evening) was my trip to the McDonald Observatory atop the adjacent mountains. The facility is operated by the University of Texas and includes four optical telescopes as well as radio telescopes in the lower valley. A tour during the daylight hours of the largest of the four optical telescopes, together with lectures and other programs, played to my life-long interest in astronomy and cosmology.

Fortunately it was Tuesday, the only day of the week with a scheduled evening stargazing program. I had an opportunity to look through the reflecting telescopes at the nighttime skies and also see real-time programs of various aspects of our universe presented by a knowledgeable and engaging staff. It was a stimulating experience and an appropriate one to remember as I gazed at the cosmos on the day that would have been my dad's 93rd birthday. That night I camped at Fort Davis State Park, one of the nicest state parks I had yet seen, on probably the coldest of my camping nights. It wasn't easy getting out of the sleeping bag the following morning!

I returned to the town of Fort Davis, foraging about the few shops there, intent on getting myself a cowboy hat -- not one from a souvenir shop or a clothier, but an authentic, pre-owned one, if possible! And, voila, there was a western hat factory/store in town that made felt cowboy hats. They also had a collection of used, consigned cowboy hats placed on display by local cowboys. These hats looked as though they'd been through many cattle drives and sold for $150 each! I was flabbergasted to learn this was considered a bargain and according to the proprietor, one could pay twice that on an e-bay auction site. I did not find one that I liked well enough and that fit me, nor was I willing to part with $150 to own one of these relics. The owner offered to custom make me a hat according to my specifications, including a weathered look, for $350. Despite a persistent effort on my part, none of my previous negotiating skills, honed from my career in the diamond business, could effect any change in the prices for the new or used hats. So my quest continued.

A year later I returned to Fort Davis with my three grandsons and we went to the same store. The used hats were still there, but no longer for sale......at any price! Instead, there was a "memorial wall" with these hats prominently displayed in memory of their former owners.

As I drove north over the Davis Mountains toward Guadalupe National Park, there had been a light snowfall, evidenced by the patches I saw along the road's higher elevations. A second night of camping in a nearby state park in the cold mountain air encouraged me to get an early start for Guadalupe National Park. On route I made a fuel stop at a gas station/general store in Kent. While in the store, I noticed a couple of used cowboy hats similar to those I had seen in Fort Davis. After some modest negotiating with the proprietor, I purchased a dark brown, well worn symbol of the American West for $15, a ninety-per-cent discount from the Fort Davis store price. A hydrogen peroxide disinfectant rinse of the inside headband was all that was needed to make the hat user friendly and I proudly wore my "new" cowboy hat thereafter.

I enjoyed a hearty breakfast in Van Horn before continuing to Guadalupe National Park through an area of ranches spread out along the low-lying plains. The backdrop is the rugged Guadalupe Range, whose centerpiece is Guadalupe Peak, at 8,750 feet the highest point in Texas. I was surrounded by these mountains, and the land form was reminiscent of the Ngorongoro Crater in Tanzania, East Africa. With clear blue skies and temperatures of 60 degrees at 10:00 a.m., it promised to be another lovely day in the Southwest. I arrived at the Visitor Center at 9:00 a.m., having picked up another hour upon entering Mountain Time. After viewing an interpretative slide presentation, I drove to McKittrick Canyon where I parked my car at the trailhead and embarked on a seven-mile, round-trip hike to the Grotto and hunter's cabin in the canyon.

It is required on such trails to register at the trailhead by signing in with a departure time. This is done for the safety of hikers, so that the park staff can account for their whereabouts. This hike was not very challenging with its modest elevation changes, but after two miles I was in an area where the elevation of the surrounding mountains was upwards of 6,000 feet. The trail ended at a grotto carved out of the soft limestone formations with a hunter's cabin nearby. At this point, on a grassy patch of land adjacent to the cabin with sunshine, mild temperatures, and peaceful surroundings, I dozed easily. Only after my thirty-minute nap was interrupted by a mule deer whose path I apparently occupied, did I return to the trailhead, grateful it was a deer and not a mountain lion passing through.

Knowing my next destination was Carlsbad Caverns, the immensely popular national park forty miles north into New Mexico, I wanted to arrive before the upcoming weekend crowds. Reluctantly I departed Guadalupe. after only one day and arrived at White's City, a complex of motels, restaurants, arcades, and souvenir shops along I-180 at the turnoff to the cavern's entrance seven miles away.

Following a good night's rest, I arrived at the Visitor Center of Carlsbad Caverns National Park as it opened, looking forward to a full day of cave exploration and touring. I followed a self-guided route through the cavern's natural entrance down a steep path leading 750 feet below the surface. Because of the relative purity of the cavern's limestone, the formations are essentially colorless; but the lack of color is more than compensated for by the spectacular shapes of the formations. Stalactites, stalagmites, columns, and variations thereof continually awed me with their ornate character. It was an especially rewarding two-hour walk through the huge chambers. I recalled reading about and seeing pictures of Carlsbad Caverns when I was twelve years old, hoping for a chance to see them in person. It only took me a half century to realize that dream!

I had made a reservation for a guided tour of the Lower Cave, an unimproved portion of the caverns requiring helmets, lanterns, gloves, and two park ranger guides. Our six-member team went that afternoon, outfitted as noted, through an area of the caverns devoid of manmade stairs, walkways, or lighting. The three-and-one-half-hour exploration provided a rudimentary feel for what caving is like, and I found it a thoroughly enjoyable and exciting experience. During a repeat visit a year later with my three grandsons, this guided, cave tour was the highlight of their trip!

With my visit to Carlsbad Caverns concluded, I drove northward past the town of Carlsbad and settled into a tent at the Brackenville Lake State Park on another chilly evening. I looked forward to an early start the next day to the White Sands National Monument, 150 miles to the northwest. I departed the park at daybreak and drove across the Sacramento Mountain Range toward Alamogordo.

I arrived at the National Space Museum in Alamogordo, site of our county's first atomic bomb detonation, adjacent to White Sands National Monument.

During a one-hour museum tour, I enjoyed the discussion on the history and technology of the facility with an enthusiastic and knowledgeable volunteer who been involved in the space-related operations of this area since he moved here fifty years ago.

The White Sands National Monument is an uninterrupted expanse of 600,000 acres of white sand stretching out like huge waves across the landscape. I drove seven miles into the sand area where the road ended at the Alkali Lake trailhead. From that point there was a five-mile walking loop across the dunes, with the only markers being orange colored poles set in the sand at lengthy intervals. With no other hikers around, the scene had an isolated and forbidding aura to it. I felt I was on the movie set of *Lawrence of Arabia*. Brilliant white gypsum sand extended 360 degrees around, framed by distant snowcapped mountains on the horizon. I imagined what the trek is like in the summer months with temperatures well above the pleasant 70 degrees I experienced.

Fig. 16 - Picnic/rest area at entrance to White Sands National Monument, NM

After completing my desert foray, I drove 120 miles to Silver City, an old frontier town in western New Mexico where silver was discovered a century and a half ago. The breadth and diversity of the landscape in the region continued to amaze me. On my earlier drive from Carlsbad to White Sands, I traversed the Lincoln National Forest in the Sacramento Mountain Range at elevations of 8,000 feet with abundant snow and temperatures in the upper 30s for much of my drive.

After an overnight stay in Silver City, I continued north to Socorro. Along the way, I stopped at the site of the VLA, or Very Large Array, a group of radio telescopes in the mountains sixty miles west of Socorro. The weather forecast indicated severe storms were due in the area. This would be of particular concern because the roads for the next hundred miles are through the mountains, up and down hairpin turns, with many areas vulnerable to rock slides. I was nervous about the storm prospects but decided to continue anyway.

By early afternoon I was a half hour from VLA and I was through the mountain passes. The precarious ride seemed like it would never end! The terrain and drop-offs were such that I was forced to keep both hands on the steering wheel and my eyes firmly watching the road. Once back on level land, I stopped in the hamlet of Maglenta at an ice cream shop to settle myself with a vanilla milkshake. After passing through a couple of small ghost towns, I arrived at the VLA facility.

This is one of the world's premier radio telescope sites. There is a total of twenty-seven dishes arranged in a "Y" pattern across the grounds that permit the radio wave viewing of an area of the universe equivalent to that which would be seen by a single dish the size of metropolitan Washington DC. Several scenes from the movie *Contact* starring Jody Foster were filmed there.

Concluding my self-guided visit at the VLA facility, I continued to the town of Socorro, arriving just ahead of a severe front of thunderstorms. It was Saturday evening in Socorro and for my "night on the town" I went to a movie theater, circa 1950, to see *Million Dollar Baby*. The next morning I attended church services at the San Miguel Mission. This attractive adobe church was built in the late 1500s, and some of the original portions of the structure remain to this day. The Catholic service was conducted in Spanish and I spent the time in prayer and thanksgiving for my safe, enjoyable, and meaningful journey to this point.

From here I continued northeast seventy-five miles to Albuquerque. I checked into a motel in the Old Town district of Albuquerque near the Atomic Energy Museum and the New Mexico Museum of Natural History, both of which I planned to visit the following morning. That afternoon was the final round of the Doral Open in which Tiger Woods was paired with Phil Mickelson. Tiger managed a one-stroke victory that returned him to number one in the world golf rankings. I enjoyed watching golf for a change since it is something that has not been on my mind for the past few months.

The next day I toured the Natural Atomic Museum and the New Mexico Museum of Natural History. The latter maintained an extensive collection of dinosaur fossils from the region, and the presentation of New Mexico's cultural and geological history was exceptional. Before going to Santa Fe, I visited the Sandia Peak Tramway, a three-mile cable ride to the summit of Sandia Peak, which at 10,400 feet afforded a panoramic view of the valley below.

A pleasant alternative to the I-25 highway between Albuquerque and Santa Fe was the Turquoise Trail, which passed through several small mining towns. A fourteen-mile stretch known as the Sandia Crest National Scenic Byway climbs 4,000 feet through the Cibola National Forest to the top of the 10,700-ft. Sandia Crest through four life zones; this is equivalent to driving from New Mexico to Canada's Hudson Bay. In other words, there is different vegetation and animal life belts that vary with altitude and latitude; within this short drive, such changes occur four times. The lowest level is represented by a desert environment while at the summit of the road one finds the Hudsonian Life zone characterized by spruce-alpine firs and associated life forms.

I arrived at the outskirts of Santa Fe at the end of the day and I checked into a motel. Since the legislature was in session (Santa Fe is the state capital) and there was a sizable contingent of ski vacationers, rooms were at a premium.

The next morning I continued to downtown Santa Fe for an early check-in at the *Anasazi Inn*, a small, upscale hotel near the central plaza, ideally located for walking about Santa Fe. I enjoyed a stroll around the area and visited a few galleries and museums in the historic plaza area. Lee, the brother-in-law of my good friend Marc, moved to the area a few years ago from Boston, and we met for a delightful lunch at the

Georgia O'Keefe Museum Café. I commented on the large number of art galleries and studios throughout Santa Fe, and Lee noted that despite Santa Fe's relatively small population, it is the country's third largest art market; only New York and Los Angeles exceed it. After lunch, I had an enriching tour of the O'Keefe Museum; particularly appealing to me were the photo exhibits of Georgia O'Keefe's mentor and husband, Alfred Stieglitz. I also visited the nearby Palace of Governors, the oldest public building in the United States. I concluded my day's activities with a lengthy walk to Canyon Street, lined with Santa Fe's most expensive art galleries and studios. I dined that evening on a mesquite grilled rib eye steak (excellent and expensive) in *Anasazi's* main dinning room before retiring for the night

The next morning, I drove to the Hill Museums on the outskirts of Santa Fe where there were several museums depicting the history and culture of the Native Americans of the region. The Culture Museum had a Navajo exhibit that verbalized their response to winter. I thought it appropriate to quote and forward the ancient verse to my family and friends back home who were struggling through a tough New England winter.

The saying is: "The Navajo people learned a long time ago that winter is the ultimate test of applied faith. Winter seems harsh but at its heart, we plant a seed of knowledge. Knowing that winter is a time of transformation, the Navajo people retreat into the warmth of hogans, tell stories of creation, sing songs, and utter long prayers. We also play shoe and string games. These are all activities which nourish the human spirits and allow the soul to attain staying power. When winter arrives, the Elders teach the sacred knowledge to younger generations so that we, the people, may continue. Winter allows for reflection, correction, and growth."

From Santa Fe I drove to Los Alamos, where our country's atomic energy program was developed during the early 1940s. The Bradbury Science Museum had a significant collection of artifacts and archived material relating to our atomic age, much of it comparable to exhibits I had previously seen at the National Atomic Museum in Albuquerque.

Next I passed through a Pueblo Indian reservation, before settling into a motel in the town of Cuba. From there I went to Chaco Culture National Monument and embarked on a three-mile hike in the canyons where the indigenous Pueblo Indians built extensive residential structures throughout the four-corner region of Arizona, New Mexico, Utah, and Colorado during the period 900 to 1200 A.D.

My walk took me through and around several of the ruins, as well as to cliffs where many pictographs remain on the sandstone walls. The drama of those surroundings, together with another day of bright blue skies and warm temperatures, made for a contemplative atmosphere. With no one else around and in the solitude of these ancient Indian sites, my thoughts turned to Loretta. Her great, great paternal grandfather was born a Blackfeet Indian and her own black hair and diminutive figure modestly suggested that connection. I recall a visit we made many years ago to the Anasazi ruins in northern Arizona. While touring the site, I chided Loretta that she may be on her ancestral lands. In fact, the Blackfeet homelands were in the northern plain states.

Fig. 17 - Pueblo Indian civilization remains at Chaco Culture National Historic Park, Chaco Canyon, NM

This was yet another occasion in which I especially missed my wife of forty-three years. I realized how important, even necessary, this journey was for me to be able to move forward with my life in a healthy, productive way.

From Chaco Canyon it was a short ride to the Aztec ruins (misnamed by the early settlers), and located outside Farmington, NM, where I briefly surveyed the ancient site before continuing north to Durango, CO. I intended to camp at Mesa Verde National Park; my drive through Durango was intended only to stock up on supplies for my camping over the next several days. With temperatures expected to fall to the upper teens during the night, I was reluctant to camp out.

Attracted by the charm of Durango, in particular its restored downtown and operating railroad, reminiscent of the late 1800's when it was a bustling railroad hub, I decided to stay the evening and booked a room at the historic *Strathmore Hotel*. Situated in the center of town, the *Strathmore* retained the elegance of a bygone era, and its trendy lounge and restaurant attracted an equally fashionable crowd. A late afternoon walk around town afforded me an opportunity to go to a few outfitting stores to replace my broken pedometer and LED headlamp. That evening I dined on farm-raised elk at the hotel's popular restaurant (less tasty than beef, but tender and lean).

I conversed with family and friends that evening, who confirmed what the TV and radio had been reporting: New England was being battered by a brutal mid-winter snow storm with high winds and zero-degree temperatures. Despite my reprieve from that New England wallop, I empathized with my family who were enduring the trying conditions.

On my walk the next morning I noted that the Durango Film Festival was being held over the next few days. With rain forecasted later in the week and to take advantage of the current fine weather, I chose to depart for Mesa Verde National Park, a twenty-mile drive along a precipitous roadway toward the mountains of Mesa Verde. The snow-capped mountains in the distance sharply contrasted with the blue skies and created a visual masterpiece. At Mesa Verde the ancient Puebloans built their dwellings in the cliff-rock alcoves that rise 2,000 feet above the Montezuma Valley. Archaeologists have located more than 600 of them, dating from A.D. 550, with forty of the cliff dwellings visible from the park roads and open to the public.

My visit to Mesa Verde included a walking tour of the park's best preserved site near the Chapin Mesa Museum and park headquarters. This time of year, with few tourists and a reduced park staff, the road leading to the Cliff Palace, the most magnificent of the park's dwellings, was closed to the general public. However, I wanted to see those ruins and decided to hike to the site, four miles down the road. I was rewarded for my perseverance. The park director was showing his guests the Cliff

Palace, and maybe because he felt sorry for me having to walk to the site as he passed me in his SUV, he allowed me to tour the dwellings. That walk, as well as another one along the canyon rim, afforded me spectacular views of the cliff dwellings set into the opposite side of the canyon and were the highlight of my Mesa Verde visit.

It was too cold for me to camp in Mesa Verde for the night so I returned down the mountains to the town of Cortez. It was late afternoon and an hour ride to Monticello, Utah. Since Canyonland National Park was only fourteen miles away, I continued my drive, intending to camp that night in the park. I didn't realize it was another thirty-four miles after the Canyonland turnoff to the park's entrance. The drive was on a remote, winding road with several hairpin turns, continually ascending and descending over and around the region's sandstone formations, brilliantly colored by the setting sun. It was a long drive, made all the more so by my concern that it was getting dark and I had no idea where I'd be sleeping that night.

I finally arrived at the park's entrance (closed) and went directly to the campground four miles away. The sixteen sites were all occupied, but a second campground nearby had a vacancy. Under the lights of my flashlight, lantern, and headlamp, I pitched my tent, dined on sardines and crackers, and updated my journal with the day's events before retiring after a very long and tiring day.

Bright sunny skies greeted me the next morning and I was anxious to start the day's activities. I was, however, becoming increasingly annoyed with the difficulty I've had in getting a decent night's sleep in my tent. I couldn't figure it out because I had no problem getting to sleep, only remaining so for more than a couple of hours was difficult. This contrasts with my motel stays where I invariably slept right through the night.

The Green and Colorado Rivers flow together in the heart of Canyonlands National Park and are responsible for carving out the mazes of canyons with their sandstone pillars and other spectacular shapes that define the region. I stopped at the Visitor Center for a trail map before heading out on a six-mile round trip hike through the canyons via the Elephant Hill Trail. It was an exhilarating hike up to a ridge and over to the opposite side of the canyon to view a panorama of weathered spires of sandstone known as The Needles. At the conclusion of my three-hour hike, I enjoyed my typical trail lunch: Gatorade, peanut butter crackers, Hershey bar, and an apple. Returning to my car at the trailhead, I continued to Moab an hour away and near Arches National Park, which is another part of southern Utah's extended canyon country, carved and shaped by aeons of weathering and erosion.

I passed through Moab on to Arches National Park with the intent of camping there for the night. Upon checking with the Visitor Center, however, I learned the fifty-two camping sites were filled that evening, in part because there was a road marathon going on that weekend in Moab. I backtracked for ten miles to Moab where I checked into the *Moab Inn* before returning to Arches. It was an easy drive through the park and for the next three hours I alternated walking and driving to see much of what the park had to offer, which was spectacular canyon topography. The park contains over 2,000 natural arches, the greatest concentration in the world. With giant balanced rocks, spires, and pinnacles, all with their red sandstone profiles set against a deep blue, cloudless sky late in the day, the scenery was breathtaking.

There were several hiking trails a short distance from the main road and I chose a couple of the shorter ones to get away from the Saturday crowd and photograph the spectacular formations. Quite frankly, after my lengthy hike that same morning in Canyonlands, I felt all hiked out. Nonetheless, I enjoyed the drive through the park and returned to my motel, showered, and took a walk about the bustling main street of Moab.

Fig. 18 – Wind-sculpted sandstone formations at Arches National Park, UT

Having read about an upscale restaurant, *Central Café*, in Moab, and after two days of eating out of my car inventory, I was looking forward to a good meal. The *Central Café* met all of my expectations and more. Served in a casual outdoor courtyard setting, my rib eye steak and accompaniments ranked up there with my dinner at *Boudreau's* in San Antonio earlier in this trip. Wonderfully tender and tasty was the beef, complemented with a half bottle of a full bodied cabernet, followed by frozen yogurt and cognac; a satisfying end to a long day. The next morning I attended an Episcopal service, once again giving thanks to God for my safety thus far, my health, and also for the continued good health of family and friends.

From Moab I continued northward to Capitol Reef National Park, a maze of canyons, massive domes, and cliffs. Here I had to address an issue that would affect the itinerary for my forthcoming visit to Death Valley National Park in southern California. With extensive rains in that region over the past several months, there was a profusion of wild flowers throughout the area, especially in Death Valley. The display was considered a once-in-a-century happening that I wanted to witness and photograph. Furthermore, I was informed by a park ranger at Arches that the flowers would be at their peak bloom for only another week, so I decided my visits to Capitol Reef, Bryce, and Zion National Parks would be relatively brief.

After picking up a guide map for the hiking trails on arrival at Capitol Reefs, I proceeded on an ambitious nine-mile hike through Spring Canyon, following a deep gorge along the Fremont River between very narrow, steeply-sided canyons. Hiking in such ravines can be dangerous, as any rain quickly produces a torrent of water streaming through the canyon. Fortunately, with a cloudless sky, such a scene was unlikely and my three hour hike ended comfortably.

After a shorter hike in the Capitol Gorge section of the park where ancient Indian petroglyphs of human figures were carved into the canyon walls, I left the park for Bryce Canyon along a magnificent stretch of Utah's roadways. My route took me across 11,000-ft.-high Boulder Mountain, up and down narrow winding roads, and through canyons with precipitous drops on either side.

I stopped for the night at a roadside motel in the small Mormon town of Escalante, discouraged again from camping by the cold temperature at the higher elevations. I left at daybreak for Bryce Canyon and arrived shortly after the Visitor Center opened and was advised by a park ranger that Bryce would be much colder and have significantly more snow than my previous destinations because of its higher altitude (in places, over

9,000 feet). The temperature hovered in the mid 20s with packed snow banks several feet above my head in many places. Yet the roads were clear and there was a bright blue sky, so I took an hour-and-a-half ride along the primary auto route within the park.

Nowhere are the erosive powers of nature more apparent than at Bryce Canyon. Its wilderness of sculptured pinnacles and spires, known as hoodoos, look like a scene from another world. I stopped at Bryce Point to photograph the expansive, naturally formed Bryce Amphitheater in the heart of the park. Along the route I took a couple of short walks but frankly, with temperatures in the twenties, windy conditions, and snow covered trails, they were not particularly enjoyable.

Along one of the overlooks I shared a few pleasant and humorous minutes with a small group of Japanese tourists who were intent on taking pictures of one another. I recalled a few Japanese words and phrases from my years traveling to Japan on business and offered to take their group picture. They heartedly agreed and I requested they take my photo as well. It was then that one of the Japanese ladies wanted her picture taken with me. She explained, in her best English, there were three women and only two men in their group and it would be nice if I could join them for the rest of their trip. Mmmm! I wasn't sure what to make of her suggestion, but politely declined and, amid laughter, we bid a warm farewell to each other (sayonara), and I concluded my half-day visit to Bryce.

Two hours later I arrived at Zion National Park, which was several thousand feet lower than Bryce, and considerably warmer. Carved by the Virgin River in Utah's high plateau country, Zion's character is defined by sheer cliffs dropping some 3000 feet, massive buttresses, deep alcoves, and gorges; the scale is immense. An interesting and notable difference between Zion (and other canyon parks like Grand Canyon and Bryce) is that with the latter two the observer views the parks primarily from above, that is, looking down or into the canyon areas. With Zion the visitor enters into the lower portion of the canyon where the Visitors' Center and campground is located. One sees Zion's majestic features from the bottom looking up.

With several hours of daylight remaining I drove along the scenic loop where there were numerous stopping points with trailheads for hikes of varying lengths and difficulty. Given the time of day, I chose a couple in the two-to-four-mile range. One of the walks was a four-mile round trip beginning at the base of the canyon along the Virgin River on a paved path with a good perspective of the canyon's geology. My second walk was up the canyon ledge for an overview of the canyons. Though shorter, it was more strenuous and photographically rewarding.

Fig. 19 - Shear cliffs characterize the rugged natural beauty of Zion National Park, UT

Tenting that evening was a bit uncomfortable with the outside temperature at daybreak down to 30°F. It was March 15th, well before Zion's busy tourist season, yet there were a fair number of people there. Judging by the expansive Visitor Center and overall infrastructure, including a large number of buses on site used to shuffle tourists around the park during peak vacation times, it was obvious that Zion accommodates hordes of visitors in those periods. I prefer to imagine and not experience that scene!

I broke camp at daybreak and headed toward Death Valley National Park, anxious to get there while the floral display was at its peak. It was a six-hour drive on the interstate including stops, and it was one of the few times that I departed from my secondary road regimen. The mileage seemed more than I could accomplish in that time frame, but with freeway speeds of 85-90 mph, distances appeared to shrink. Along the way I passed the town of St. George, noted for its grand, cathedral-like St. George Church of the Latter Day Saints, which dominates the skyline. It serves as a regional gathering place for the greater Mormon community.

My final stop in Nevada was the town of Pahrump near the California border, where I expected to have several rolls of film developed at a local Wal-Mart while getting gas and lunch before continuing to Death Valley. While there, I noticed a couple of billboards that interrupted my travel plans. Willow Creek Golf Course was enticingly described on one of them. It was a sunny, warm day, about 1 o'clock, and I could make a case for a fast walking round of golf. The second billboard espoused the pleasures of a ranch located fifteen minutes from town. In Nevadan parlance, "ranch" is the socially preferred name for bordello (whorehouse), which are legal enterprises in that state.

What I am about to relate is a totally honest recounting of the afternoon's events. Before continuing, I should tell you that when I returned home and described this same scenario to my friends, I posed the following trivia question: of the three places, Death Valley, Willow Creek Golf Course, and Madam X's Ranch (renamed in this story) - - which did I choose? No one answered correctly because I went to all three! But my follow-up question was: at which one did I remain? Now it's not so simple.

I'll explain. The golf course was my first stop, but its appearance did not impress me and, anyway, I didn't want to spend three hours or more banging a white ball around some converted desert land. Madam X's brothel was close by, and since I have NEVER been to one, I thought it would be an opportunity to expand my sphere of knowledge!

After a fifteen-minute drive on an isolated (at times, gravel) road, I nervously pulled up to a trailer-like building situated away from other commercial establishments. Two other cars were in the parking lot. I walked through a wrought iron gate leading to an ornate front door. On entering I was greeted by an attractive, older (my age group), statuesque woman with long blond hair. She was the madam (or so I assumed) and her demeanor was business-like, even abrupt, as she seated me in a darkened room. She first asked if I had been there before; I said I hadn't and, in fact, added that I'd never been to a whorehouse in Nevada or elsewhere. I was then told that several girls would be paraded before me and I could select one. Rather coldly and emphatically the madam said that all prices for services must be negotiated with the girl and that would be done in a separate room. At this point I was concerned that once taking that next step I'd be committed, at least fiscally, to something, so I started to leave.

But I was informed that I could leave anytime without cost so long as no services were performed, so I remained. Several girls were paraded before me in the darkened room. Having come in from the bright, noon-day sun, my eyes were still adjusting to the dim lighting. Even so, the selection was not impressive. I did choose a dark-haired Eurasian girl, probably in her early 20s, and I was led to a small bedroom with all the accompaniments the girls apparently use to ply their trade: creams, oils, and, of course, condoms were most visible. Thus far I had not committed to anything. I sat next to her desk and was politely given a menu to peruse. That's right. Like a restaurant, except in place of soup, salad, steak, seafood, etc., there were items descriptive of a variety of sexual favors at prices *starting at* $400, a la carte!

We discussed the various choices in casual and pleasant terms. I said I'd been camping for several days and first needed a bath. Her recommendation was the "total bath and body treatment" package for $1,500. Comfortably in control of my urges, I said I was in a hurry to get to Death Valley, so how long would it take? She said I could be out of there in an hour. Imagine, one hour of her time for $1,500! A pretty good hourly rate, even for a top-notch lawyer! Thanks, but no thanks! At that point I said, "I'd rather stop on my way back when I'll have more time." My comments elicited several teasingly complementary comments from her in an effort to keep me interested, but I proceeded to politely extricate myself without cost from the negotiations. I then proceeded unimpeded by delay, expense, or regret to my original destination. As an aside, and most emphatically, the cost of services was not a factor in my decision to take a pass on the offerings!

By mid-afternoon, I arrived at Death Valley and was welcomed by the warmest weather I'd had since Cumberland Island, SC, back in January. As I entered the park, the outside temperature was 78° F with sunny hazy skies, and my focus was immediately turned to the plethora of desert gold flowers in full bloom all about me. It was a colorful scene of seemingly endless fields and hills dotted with yellow and purple against a backdrop of snow- capped Telescope Peak, Death Valley's highest point at 11,050 feet.

Fig. 20 - Floral display at its finest in the desert of Death Valley, CA

Equally visible, but not nearly as attractive, were the cars lined up
on either side of the road, whose occupants with camera and tripods
in hand were intent on capturing the floral display. After taking some
of my own photos and concerned about getting a campsite that late
in the day, I continued to Furnace Creek, the principal tourist center
of Death Valley. There, a spring-fed oasis supports the Furnace Creek
Ranch golf course, Visitor Center, lodge, restaurant, and campground.
The golf course is the world's lowest in elevation above sea level, so the
player's ball's flight will be reduced by the relatively higher air density.
Perhaps this offers a good excuse for those disappointed in their driving
distances!

By the time I arrived there were no vacancies at the lodge and
campground. There was a tent overflow area that was nothing more
than a gravel parking lot opposite the Furnace Creek campground. I had
little choice, but in the process of setting up my tent one of my fiberglass
tent poles broke, rendering my tent useless. Only later in Santa Monica,

CA, was I able to locate and purchase a set of higher quality aluminum poles that served me well for the balance of my trip. Meanwhile with no replacement poles available at Furnace Creek, I figured that since I had not been sleeping well in my tent, I could do no worse in my car. And I didn't.

I was up at what I thought was 6:00 a.m., unaware I had passed through another time zone and it was only 5:00 a.m. I drove to Badwater, which at 282 feet below sea level is the lowest point in the Western Hemisphere. Here was a menagerie of rock salt pinnacles that formed as water evaporated through the salty crust; it is known as "Devil's Golf Course." I photographed the surreal landscape beneath the rising sun and returned to Furnace Creek to "buy" myself a shower, which is the protocol in this area since the campgrounds do not have showers. A three-dollar ticket entitled me to the use of the poolside showers at the lodge. After that I took a casual drive through the park, stopping off at selected areas for short walks to various sites. I also did a strenuous hike to the Keane Mine, an abandoned silver and gold mine 1,500 feet up from the basin, and a very steep ascent. Despite the difficulty of the hike, it was worthwhile as I saw several abandoned mine shafts, as well as equipment used in the late 19th century to haul ore from the mines.

Backtracking toward Furnace Creek, I visited the Harmony Borax Works, site of the richest fields of crude ore yet discovered for the naturally occurring mineral composed of sodium, boron, oxygen, and water. California businessman William Coleman first filed claims for the Death Valley deposits in the 1880s for the product that became a staple multi-purpose cleaner for households around the world. A museum on the Furnace Creek premises houses a collection of memorabilia from the early days of the borax mining operation.

Encompassing 3.4 million acres, Death Valley is the largest of our country's national parks south of Alaska. Traversing it was a lengthy ordeal and I concentrated on the areas that best represented the park's diversity. The congestion and activity at Furnace Creek reminded me of Bay Street, Watch Hill, on a summer weekend, but once I got away from that area, there was a desolation and vastness I came to appreciate. Death Valley is the lowest, hottest, and driest area in the Western Hemisphere. Despite that fact, when the park was ravaged by flash floods from heavy downpours over the winter of 2004, some roads were washed out, a Visitor Center was destroyed, and at one point, tourists were evacuated from the park. Death Valley is a most unusual place; the more time I spent there, the more I treasured the experience.

Later in the afternoon I left the park by detouring several miles over a deeply rutted, dirt road to the former mining, now ghost town of Ballarat. Many mining implements and work tools were scattered across the landscape surrounding a small dilapidated store that sold only soda pop. A lone man who mirrored his surroundings appeared outside and collected my soda money while conversing about the town's history. A tin can in his hand labeled "donations" was intended for visitors (at the moment I was the only one) to pay for his guide services. It was an interesting side trip and I took several black and white photos of the antiquated machinery scattered over the grounds, including a junked pick-up truck that purportedly once belonged to cult figure and mass murderer, Charles Manson.

Fig. 21 – Man-made relics litter the ghost town of Ballarat, CA

From Ballarat I continued south through the mineral mining town of Trona and ended up in Ridgecrest, bordering the Mojave Desert, where I spent the night. The following morning I continued on a leisurely drive toward Santa Monica, interrupted only when I noticed the spectacular canyon landscape of Red Rock State Park off to my right. Detouring though the park, I thought the expansive, private campsites with a backdrop of red rock canyons and cliffs collectively made for as fine an outside venue as I'd seen thus far!

My day's drive ended in Mission Hills, twenty-five miles from Santa Monica. Here I spent the evening, and after a sumptuous St. Patrick's Day meal of corned beef and cabbage at a popular Irish Pub, I re-packed my bags and otherwise prepared for my flight back home in a few days. I made reservations at a motel in Santa Monica where I would meet up with my granddaughter Arielle, a second year student at Santa Monica

College and an aspiring filmmaker. She is a beautiful, curly-haired young lady with an infectious smile and vibrant personality and I was so looking forward to seeing her again. I arrived in Santa Monica the following morning and we subsequently spent an enjoyable weekend together, on and about the beaches, piers, and streets of Venice and Santa Monica, basking in the delightful Southern Californian weather and catching up on each other's lives. I departed LAX to Connecticut on the first day of spring, expecting to return in a week to continue my adventure.

The lengthy flight home afforded me an opportunity to revisit the second leg of my journey, which was markedly different from the first. The first phase was less about the landscape and outdoor pursuits than about American history and culture. Yes, there were regions of natural beauty: the Outer Banks, Cumberland Island, and the primeval southern swamplands. But what I remember most is the role of the region and its place in our history.

My route from San Antonio westward took on a very different cast: it captivated me with the unimaginable expanse of our great Southwest, showcased by its snowcapped mountains, multi-colored wind/water sculpted canyons, and high and low desert terrain. I envisioned this kaleidoscope of scenes as the "southwest corner of heaven."

Driving through and hiking in the national parks was as much a spiritual experience as it was a physical challenge. At times along my hikes, alone and surrounded by incredible scenery, I felt inspired to delve into the questions I had raised for myself at the outset of this journey. Those hikes into the less traveled areas of the parks and reserves were peaceful and stimulating, precious times for me to be appreciative of my past, thankful for the present, and enthusiastic about my future.

My impressions along this leg of my journey were influenced less by the people and more by the land. I valued my conversations and interaction with people I met en route, but my overwhelming sense of this part of America suggests it is defined by the landscape rather than its people. I say this despite the impressive culture of the indigenous Puebloans, whose ancient dwellings remain to this day and whose influence is expressed in the art of the Southwest.

This vast and rugged territory is attracting increasing numbers of easterners of all generations to its benign climate and open spaces. Vibrant, career oriented, outdoor-loving youths lent a dynamic air to the area. Recreational opportunities abound and with those activities come the jobs and infrastructure needed to support a growing population. Although the region may be geologically and spiritually mature, I see its economic and social core as just moving beyond childhood, eager and intent in its adolescence to become a productive adult.

LEG THREE: WEST, NORTHWEST

I returned to Santa Monica, again joining up with Arielle who I invited to accompany me for a day hike to the Channel Islands National Park off the coast of southern California. This group of five islands, including the surrounding waters of the National Marine Sanctuary, protects and supports a variety of wildlife. A relatively new national park (est. 1980), The Channel Islands function as a refuge for several marine and land species and protect the giant kelp forests of the surrounding undersea environment.

We joined a boat excursion from Ventura for the twenty-one mile trip to Santa Cruz, the largest of the islands. After disembarking, we headed out on our own for a two-hour hike among the hills and meadows of Santa Cruz to a cliff promenade, Potato Harbor, which encompasses the meeting of land and sea in spectacular fashion. The sharply defined cliffs plummeted down to the crashing waves of the blue Pacific and lent a look to the landscape reminiscent of the Galapagos chain of islands. This was a special place to spend my last day in southern California with Arielle. Our boat returned from the island at the end of a long and rewarding day; it was a day I know we will both cherish. Many months later I received the following commentary from Arielle in which she shares her impressions of our day in the Channel Islands:

Fig. 22 - Granddaughter Arielle poses along a cliffside trail on Santa Cruz Island within Channel Islands National Park, CA

"The café down the street packed sandwiches, ham and cheese and a California Caprice. Before dawn they found themselves in our backpacks and we found ourselves on the road toward a harbor about an hour north. Here we would catch a ferry that would take us to the largest and most hikeable of the Channel Islands, Santa Cruz. While I knew my grandfather had done his research, I also knew that having tickets for this boat was special, usually booked long in advance, and we were fortunate to find our way into a completely unpredicted adventure.

Arriving early, we ate a quick breakfast overlooking a harbor reminiscent of New England. Being still new to the west, I don't believe I had fully anticipated the change. My grandfather's trip here continued a long tradition of our history together which included being by the sea, ships, and traveling. All of this provided a certain comfort and familiarity that my life in California had not yet brought.

Reading of the problems with wild boar and the warnings of hanta virus frightened me. I felt that Santa Cruz, while open to visitation, remained in its wild, untamed state. The ferries came in and out twice a day, leaving a large chunk of time on the island, no matter how wild it turned out to be.

As we pulled into the harbor, both of us having recently visited South America could have sworn we were back there. The yellow cliffs against the horizon, the crashing crystal waves, the feeling of expanse, all led to our feelings of having been transported beyond California and into somewhere much more foreign.

We hiked the upper ridge of the island, ate lunch, took photographs, and talked, but most memorable to me was when we ventured off the path. We drifted into a yellow field by a stream and laid in what seemed to be the brightest and most energizing sun I'd ever felt. Falling into a deep nap proved that the peace of Santa Cruz had spread to me. I no longer feared the feral pigs, but instead, trusted the island to protect me while I slept.

In a strange and unpredictable irony the trip to Santa Cruz returned me to feelings of comfort, long tangents of home and at the same time whisked me into a magical land of the unknown, a land that beautifully brings you whatever you choose to bring to it. Our unexpected journey left me knowing that just off the coast of southern California, not far from what I now call home, is a beautiful and mythic escape available to me anytime the L.A. landscape grows tiresome."

We concluded my stay with dinner that evening at a fashionable Santa Monica restaurant, and after returning to Arielle's apartment for the night, I was on the road before daybreak for the 250-mile drive north to Sequoia National Park. I left with mixed emotions: I was anxious to get on with my journey, but the weather had been magnificent and I'd really enjoyed my time with Arielle.

I arrived at the southern entrance to Sequoia National Park by noon and first went to select a tent site for my overnight stay. However, I was informed by a park ranger that with the black bears just out of hibernation, the campground was an active, bear-foraging area. Their sense of smell was especially acute during that time and it was imperative and required by law that any odorous materials, food, toiletries, and anything else be removed from my auto and placed in the bear bins at the individual camp sites. Any smells within the car would leave it vulnerable to a bear break-in.

My concern was that with my car's fully packed interior, there was no assurance I could remove all scented materials. The alternative suggested by the park ranger was that I place all the food items in the metal bin and then sleep in the car that night to protect its contents as well as the car. The rationale was that bears would be discouraged by my presence in the car and would move on. However, that remained to be seen.

Sequoia, established as a National Park at the end of the 19th century, is all about huge trees (giant sequoias 3,000 years old growing to heights near 300 feet) and vastness. Virtually the entire park is a wilderness area. A backpacker here can hike to a spot that is further from a road than any other place in the forty-eight contiguous states. While planning my hike in the foothills of the park for the following morning, I took a leisurely twenty-mile drive to Giant Forest in the higher elevations of the park to see the largest of the sequoias, including the *"General Sherman"* tree, 2,700 years old, which is the world's largest living thing by total mass. It was named after the Civil War GeneralWilliam Tecumseh Sherman by naturalist James Wolverton in 1879. I wanted to hike in the immediate area, but with a four- ft. deep snow pack and six inches of new snow having fallen the night before (and my snowshoes back home in storage), it was not a manageable option. Besides, the trail markers were buried under the snow pack, and as a lone hiker I was not about to test my sense of direction.

I was in awe of my surroundings: immense red-bark giants rising from their snow covered foundations like city skyscrapers, narrowing as they reached skyward. It was nature's living monoliths at their grandest, and I used one of my photos of the Sequoia scenery for my 2005 Christmas greeting cards. After the hairpin-filled return route from the upper regions of the park, I came back to my campsite and sardine dinner before settling into my "car/bed" and recounting the day's impressionable events and sightings in my journal.

Fig. 23 – Awe-inspiring forest giants of Sequoia National Park, CA

With my food in the campsite's bear bin, I changed into comfortable sleeping clothes and listened to an audio book of Bill Bryson's *A Walk in the Woods* which recounted his Appalachian Trail hike. Excited about the prospect of a visiting bear, I readied my camera with flash attachment and macro lens and placed it on my dashboard, expecting that if a bear should pay me a visit, it would be an up close and personal one. I also placed the ignition keys in position, should a honking horn or quick engine startup be needed. I was asleep by 10:00 p.m., but awake at midnight, 1:00, then 2:30; no doubt my anxiety was in full control of my sleep pattern. At 4:02 I was startled awake by a scratching sound on my driver's side door where my head and pillow were resting. I opened my eyes to what looked like the largest bear head I had ever seen staring directly at me, six to twelve inches from my window. With a response I will forever regret, I panicked, turned the car keys to the ignition position, and started frantically honking the horn. The bear looked in the direction of the hood and slowly meandered off. My Kodak moment of a lifetime was gone. The camera was ready but I wasn't.

Early that morning, a park ranger stopped by and said that a pickup camper fifty yards from my site had its rear cab broken into by a black bear, whether the same one or not, we'll never know. As I recounted my panicked reaction upon seeing the bear, I concluded it had a two-fold cause; first, I was startled awake, momentarily forgetting where I was. Second, and more pragmatic, the bear's head was a light honey color, more like that of a grizzly than a black bear. And that was scary! There are no grizzly bears in Sequoia, but I only found out later that a black bear's colors can range from black through degrees of brown to honey.

Hoping for another opportunity to redeem myself and capture that elusive bear image on film, I decided to spend another night at the same site. The day began under a bright sunny blue sky with perfect wind and temperature conditions. There was a trailhead near my campsite commencing an eight- mile, round-trip hike along the Marble Fort Trail leading to a spectacular mountain waterfall.

During the hike I was absorbed by the words and music of Louis Armstrong's memorable song, *What a Wonderful World*. I sang aloud the lyrics to make my presence known to any bears that may have been scavenging along the trail. And I did so with joyousness at being able to appreciate my surroundings and with sadness as thoughts turned to family and friends who have passed on. The poetry of the song seemed to mirror my mother's positive outlook on people and life. I thought those words would be an eloquent eulogy to her. Little did I realize at the time that I would be reciting them at mom's memorial service later that year. She had a massive stoke in August and died a month later, peacefully, with Doris and me at her bedside.

On a more basic survival note, I also didn't realize at the time that eight months earlier a lone hiker, Shannon Parker, was mauled by a cougar in this area of Sequoia. Ignorance is sometimes bliss!

Returning from my hike, I exited Sequoia for a drive along the scenic back roads of Three Rivers, a small town twelve miles outside the park. Nearby was the tiny hamlet of Kaweah, whose post office is considered the smallest in our country. After savoring the tranquility of the pastoral countryside, I enjoyed a native trout dinner at a streamside restaurant in Three Rivers before returning to my campsite.

The evening was one of anticipation: I prepared my camera hoping for another visit by one of the resident bears. My sleep was shallow and anxious as I awaited the bear that never showed up. I suspect that a camper with a barking dog in the same area may have thwarted any interest on the part of a bear to come calling. *Darn it...!!!*

At daybreak I departed for Yosemite National Park, 200 miles to the north. My hope for an early arrival was dashed by a road closure due to a serious auto/truck accident on the main road leading to the south entrance. Re-routing added another two hours, resulting in a mid-afternoon arrival. Yosemite is a magnet for many who gravitate to this incredibly beautiful sculpture of the American West, once described by the naturalist John Muir as "No temple made with hands can compare with Yosemite." My first priority was to secure a campsite. Several of the campgrounds were already filled to capacity, and this was the off season! On a summer day Yosemite's main campground Yosemite Valley will be jammed with twenty thousand visitors! The main roadway through the park had several disruptions and detours because of construction activity. There is also an immense infrastructure in place to serve the throngs of people who visit Yosemite during the summer months, and finding my way around was frustrating. What a traffic nightmare it must be during the busy season! An hour later I set up my tent in a campground of 100 or more sites with minimum space between them and most already occupied by campers.

Yosemite is nature at its most inspiring! Immense, steeply carved mountains of granite among green spires of sequoia and other conifers reflect much of the beauty seen by so many, including famed photographer Ansel Adams, who spent many years there. Waters falling from the rocky pinnacles seemed to be coming from the sky itself and added a dynamic dimension to the landscape.

My car again provided overnight accommodations, though I pitched my tent for a morning nap should I experience a sleep-deprived night. I was hopeful of replicating that missed Kodak moment from Sequoia. Meanwhile I spent the rest of the afternoon within Yosemite Village, an assemblage of stores, lodges, restaurants, a post office, medical and judicial offices, and a gas/service station; for all intents and purposes, it was a small town in the central valley of Yosemite. I dined that evening at the venerable *Ahwahnee Inn*, adjacent to the village. This early 20th-century lodge was built to satisfy the discriminating tastes of the rich and famous of the time and remains the premier lodge within our national park system.

At my campsite that evening, there were bears rummaging around the area, but I had no close encounters and the night proved uneventful.

I awoke at daylight and set out for what would be the most aggressive of my hikes thus far, a four-mile climb to the top of Ventura and Nevada Falls. Misting from the falls along the steep pathway made for a wet, slippery walk, but it was an exciting and challenging trek shared by only a smattering of hikers along the route.

I returned to camp several hours later in the rain, which continued throughout the day and evening. I had a productive afternoon despite the inclement weather. Of particular interest was the Ansel Adams Gallery in Yosemite Village, which housed a substantial collection of his photographs along with books and related items for purchase. Since Adams spent much of his leisure and working time at Yosemite, the gallery was as much a tribute to his photographic genius as it was to his commercial enterprise. I purchased a book of his most popular photos of our national parks as well as a biographical DVD.

My photographic interest seemed to be gravitating to black and white composition, so I especially appreciated his works. My evening was spent watching the Ansel Adams DVD while awaiting a bear visit for my "Kodak moment." Once again, despite bear activity in adjacent campsites, my mostly sleepless night in the car passed without incident, while temperatures dropped below 30° F. At daylight I located the trailhead to Mirror Lake for a pleasant hike in an area with good views of Half Dome, the huge granite monolith, which along with El Capitan and Yosemite Falls best defines the grandeur of Yosemite.

Since the inclement weather was expected to continue, I returned to camp, packed up, and departed. In fact, snow was falling heavily as I departed the park westward toward the coast. Soon, though, all precipitation ended as I continued past Napa and arrived in Healdsburg at day's end. I checked into a centrally located motel; after my first shower in several days, I attended to several overdue housekeeping and car matters before concluding the evening with a superb rib eye steak dinner at a downtown western steak house recommended by the woman in the photo section of the local drugstore.

From Healdsburg I drove west the next morning through more wine country to join Route 1 for a delightful drive northward along a beautiful portion of coastal California. With gently sloping green fields reaching to flowering precipices and spectacular drop offs to the crashing surf of the seemingly boundless Pacific, the scenery was mesmerizing. After brief stops at several state parks along the ocean drive, I arrived at the charming seaside town of Mendocino. An artists' and writers' colony par excellence, Mendocino has to be one of the most picturesque communities on the California coast. Its postcard setting has been the site for numerous film projects, most notably the television series *Murder She Wrote,* and among the town's residences is the cottage that served as home to the program's main character. After checking into a charming bed & breakfast in the heart of the village, I had a relaxing walk along the main streets lined with upscale shops, galleries, and eateries as the views westward captured the setting sun casting its orange hues across the ocean-side cliffs of Mendocino.

What began as a light dinner at the bar of the historic *Mendocino Inn* continued late into the evening after I struck up a conversation with a gentleman seated near me who operated a local art gallery. Clinton Smith was a landscape photographer for thirty-five years who once worked for Ansel Adams. As earlier noted, when visiting the gallery at Yosemite, I was enthralled with Adams' works and my discussions with Clinton regarding photography in general and Ansel Adams in particular were stimulating and educational. Despite his work with Adams, Clinton's photos were almost exclusively in color. He was of the opinion that one could not excel by doing black and white and color photography concurrently. The artist needs to see the world through a different set of eyes for each discipline, and his preference was to see it in color.

Clinton had also been a long-time participant in expeditions recreating the journey of Lewis and Clark's "Corp of Discovery" across lands acquired by President Jefferson's Louisiana Purchase in 1803. His enthusiasm in recounting the essence of their 1804-1806 journey was infectious and he encouraged me to do some further reading on the subject, specifically Steven Ambrose's *Undaunted Courage*.

I attended services at a local Catholic church the next morning. I stopped by Clinton's gallery to purchase one of his photographs of Mendocino and thank him for sharing his insights the previous evening. From there I followed Rt. 101 north, stopping often to photograph the natural beauty of the landscape defined by expansive views of the Pacific Ocean and coastal highlands to the east. I also stopped at a winery situated on a cliff promenade overlooking the Pacific Ocean where I purchased a case of wine for shipment home.

My drive was interrupted when I detoured to a roadside pizza parlor along the "Highway-of-the-Giants." I had a late lunch and watched the last several holes of the Masters Golf Tournament won by Tiger Woods in a playoff. As soon as Tiger made his winning putt, I was back on the road.

The "Highway-of-the-Giants" is the scenic roadway passing through forests of giant coast redwood trees, the largest span of these magnificent specimens anywhere in the world. In the heart of this unique area lies Humboldt Redwood State Park, a concentrated corner of redwoods and where I camped that evening. Since bears are not known to inhabit this area, I slept in my tent, this time with an air mattress (courtesy of my sister Doris), which I brought back with me hoping it would help my tent sleeping. With nighttime temperatures staying above 40° F and a soft under-bottom, I slept soundly.

I awoke to a steady rain. In the open areas, I could see the rain coming down at a reasonable clip. Yet because of the forest canopy, resulting from the extreme height and density of the redwoods under which I had pitched my tent, I could not see or feel any drops on me. My tent, while obviously damp from the humid conditions, was essentially free of any standing moisture.

Despite the rain I hiked to Founders Grove, one of the largest stands of old growth redwood forests, where one is immediately greeted by the 345-ft. Founders Tree, believed to be 1,600 years old. Several other arboreal giants rose to over 300 feet, and in the forest was a veritable graveyard of many fallen behemoths including the Dyerville redwood giant. Until toppled by a rainstorm in 1991, it was lauded as the world's tallest tree at 362 feet -- 57 feet higher than the Statue of Liberty!

A couple of miles west of Founders Grove is the Rockefeller Forest, the largest undisturbed, contiguous tract of old growth coast redwoods in existence. With the cathedral-like silence in this land of giants, the solitude of the moment, and the awesome size and beauty of the redwoods, it felt as much a spiritual journey as it was a nature walk. Surrounded by these immense living plants, my thoughts focused on the wonders of creation, and with the second anniversary of her death in a couple of months, Loretta's absence from my life. In reality, during similar, less physically-challenged hikes, it wasn't unusual for my mind to wander to the past as I recalled some of our woodland walks. There were many, sometimes with unexpected outcomes. On occasion I even managed to get us lost on hikes in Rhode Island (Great Swamp Management Area), Connecticut, (Ragged Mt.), and New York (Gilbert Lake State Park); these only the most notable that Loretta would recollect. And here I was, hiking alone with the same directional disabilities. She was most likely looking down from heaven on my less-than- responsible solo hikes saying to my dad, "Ray may be joining us sooner than we thought!"

Leaving the redwood forests, I returned to my northerly route, stopping in the city of Eureka. Once a rough area of docks from its days as an industrial port, it now bills itself as a charming and lively artist's colony with an old town flavor enhanced by the recent development of a commercial district with shops and restaurants. It was a delightful venue and a change from my forested walks. At a seafood restaurant popular with the locals I enjoyed a delectable, baked-oyster lunch. I wonder if the outcome of my Ranch experience in Nevada would have been different if oysters would have been my luncheon choice that day! Oh well, that's probably just myth anyway!

Next on Route US 101 was Redwood National Park near the northern limit of the coastal redwoods' narrow range. These trees are best appreciated by walking among them, and I began with a short tour through the Lady Bird Johnson Grove of giant redwoods where the park was dedicated in 1969. Further up the road was the Tall Trees Grove, which included the world's tallest trees at over 360 feet. From there I drove to the Elk Prairie Campground to set up my tent for an overnight stay. In a field outside my tent, as I was in the process of recording my travels, I looked out at a herd of ten elk grazing within fifty yards of my campsite. With only two other sites occupied, it was easy to appreciate the extraordinary tranquility of that moment.

The following morning I looked forward to hiking through the park and to the rugged unspoiled coast, but a heavy downpour at daybreak discouraged me. Breaking camp in the rain, I drove northward and before long the sun was shining. It is amazing how rapidly weather changes can occur here and elsewhere in the mountainous West.

Paralleling the Klamath River, my route passed through the town of Klamath where I stopped for breakfast at a roadside café. While there I noted from posters and other promotional materials that this was a prime fishing area for salmon and steelhead trout. I purchased a California fishing license and fished the local waters without success, before heading to Crescent City, the county seat and largest city in Del Norte County (just over 4,000). The foggy weather that helps the redwoods thrive makes the city gloomy and gray much of the time and it is frequently eroded by storms off the Pacific Ocean. In 1964 it was nearly destroyed by a giant tidal wave generated by the earthquake off Alaska. I fished, again without success, in Crescent City harbor while several large sea lions sunbathed nearby. Fed up with my fishing failures, I retreated to the *Chart Inn Restaurant* on the town pier where I bought a fish, a steelhead trout. While I enjoyed someone else's catch as a fish-n-chip lunch, I met the local wildlife ranger who told me the steelhead fishing should still be good along the Smith River, which runs through Jedediah Smith State Park. I opted to camp there with hopes of landing a twenty-pound trophy steelhead on my fly rod.

Jedediah Smith is another of this region's unique and beautiful state parks, located in the northern-most regions of the redwood groves. Situated within the giant redwoods and with the sparkling clear, emerald-green Smith River running through, the park is a paradise. My tent was pitched adjacent to the white, cobble-covered banks of the river where the fishing opportunities were right in front of me in a most picturesque spot. However, several hours of fishing failed to turn up any fish, steelhead or otherwise; nevertheless, it was a most pleasant activity amid peaceful and attractive surroundings as I honed my fly casting technique.

Fig. 24 - Idyllic tent site near Green River in Jehediah Smith State Park, CA

Earlier I had passed through the town of Fort Bragg, named for the Confederate General Braxton Bragg. During its long history, Fort Bragg prospered after the devastating 1906 earthquake that destroyed its main buildings and much of San Francisco. Upon its rebuilding, Fort Bragg's mills provided most of the lumber for San Francisco's reconstruction. I stopped and purchased the audio book, *Undaunted Courage*, Stephen Ambrose's classic account of the Lewis and Clark Expedition. I had since become so engrossed in their adventure that I was finding it difficult not listening to it all the time and would play the CD before bedtime as well.

I awoke to the sounds of rain on my tent, heavier and more unrelenting than the previous two nights. Once again I broke camp in the rain and continued to the coastal town of Gold Beach, OR, a mecca for fishing enthusiasts, especially during the salmon runs up the Rogue River. I arranged for a fishing guide to take me on the river that was nearing its spring Chinook salmon run. The afternoon was spent several miles up the Rogue River from Gold Beach, and it produced a lot of rain, chilly temperatures, but no fish. Frankly, sitting in a boat and being pelted by cold rain while my bait drifted down river at the end of my spinning rod did little for my spirits. Doug, my guide, had been a logger in this region several years ago, and he spoke resignedly of the changes in the landscape evident all about us. Clear cutting from logging operations left large swaths of hillsides devoid of trees in an otherwise idyllic surrounding. Despite the natural beauty of my surroundings with conifer-laden hillsides framing the fast moving, meandering Rogue River and its rapids, I was glad to be back ashore in a warm car heading north.

At day's end I checked into a roadside motel in the tiny fishing village of Port Orford to regroup after three nights of camping in California state parks. Known as the rainiest place on the Oregon coast, Port Orford is the most westerly incorporated city in the continental United States. After a few days of mostly camp meals, I was looking forward to a full dinner and boy, was I ever rewarded!

With limited restaurant choices in town and at the recommendation of the motel manager, I tried a local restaurant, *The Crazy Norwegians*, a small nondescript seafood shack in the main area of town owned and operated by a transplanted New England couple. In sparsely decorated, neat, and clean surroundings, I relished every morsel of a scrumptious dinner of clam chowder and fresh crab cakes. A crisply fresh garden salad and homemade raspberry/blackberry pie a la mode were perfect complements to this extraordinary meal.

During dinner I met and conversed with two affable couples at an adjacent table, one of whom was just moving to Port Orford from California. They invited me to join them at their home after dinner, but I declined as I was looking forward to a full night's sleep after three nights of camping. I emphatically included *Crazy Norwegians* on my list of the top ten most memorable eateries on my journey. To food critics and authors of the bible of roadside restaurants, Jan and Michael Stern, I would ask: "How did you miss this gem?"

By now I'd finished Ambrose's book and was enthusiastically looking forward to visiting the various landmarks along the Lewis & Clark route; the bicentennial of their reaching the Pacific Ocean was 2005. The personal journal of Meriwether Lewis was written with much detail and revealed an impressive breadth of knowledge of several scientific disciplines. I am sure part of my fascination with his writings was due to the fact that I was chronicling my own personal journey of discovery.

Next morning I went to a Port Orford beach where agate was commonly found on the sandy shoreline and readily accessible to beachcombers. In order to get to the beach, I was confronted with backside tidal pools a foot deep. There were no crossroads or bridging, so it was off with my shoes and socks as I sloshed through to the beach. With the cold, dark sand (water temperature along the Oregon coast remains below sixty degrees even in the summer months) my bare feet were numbing fast and my interest in collecting agate specimens quickly waning.

Then an unexpected and pleasant change of venue: I received a telephone call from a good friend while in transit. Jack is a passionate golfer whose skills on the course are exceeded only by his interest in, and appreciation for, the quality and diversity of golf courses. During our conversation he boasted that his home golf course had just been chosen by *Golf Digest* as one of the top five in Connecticut! As he continued to name the magazine's choices for top twenty-five courses in the country, we simultaneously realized the number twenty-two ranked course, Bandon Dunes, was directly ahead of me, twenty miles from my present location.

It was mid-morning under sunny skies and temperatures in the sixties as I exited Rte. 101 into the *Dunes* complex, which was composed of Bandon Dunes, its sister course, Pacific Dunes, and a third Ben Crenshaw-designed course due to open shortly. At Bandon Dunes I joined a twosome for a memorable four-hour-and-twenty-minute round on a spectacular seaside course. With a greens fee of $160 it was not an inexpensive walk, but with the spring flowers in bloom all about and magnificent coastal vistas, my failure to break 85 was of little concern. All three courses permit public play (albeit for a stiff price), but the care and conditioning is first class in every respect. I predict this golf mecca will become, in due course, as revered a golfing destination in the States as St. Andrew's is in Scotland.

I was pleased with myself for having a flexible approach to the day's possibilities and getting the most out of the opportunities. Often I have learned to "go with the moment" and embrace the experience, which has done much for my self confidence.

The afternoon drive north passed through a forty-mile length of coastline comprising huge sand dunes, Oregon's version of the Sahara. This unusual topographical feature on the Oregon coast is the Dunes National Recreation Area, which includes sand dunes soaring to 500 feet, bisecting conifer groves on one side and the ocean on the other. Private and state campgrounds were located there and are popular with visitors who come with their ATVs for dune drives. I walked along the dunes for a while and then continued to Yachets, where I checked into a roadside motel overlooking the shoreline. An onsite jacuzzi offered welcome refurbishment after my seven-mile walk around Bandon Dunes Golf Course and later the dunes themselves.

Nearby Cape Perpetua dominates this section of Oregon's four-hundred-mile, coastal Rt. 101; the road passes national forests, state parks, and awe- inspiring views of the seacoast and ocean. Perpetua towers 800 feet above the ocean, looking down on the dark brown/gray sand beach, littered with driftwood, shells, and other marine residue. Tidal pools contain piles of seashells and other tool and pottery artifacts left behind by native peoples. I was looking forward to hiking the two-mile road to the top of Cape Perpetua and the whispering Spruce Trail around the rim of the promontory the next morning.

I was up early but once again derailed from my hiking ambitions by heavy rain, so I headed out for my final day on the Oregon coast. My initial stop was at the Tillamook Cheese Factory, which offered a tour of their century- old, cheese-making process. At the factory outlet store, I purchased several pounds of cheese varieties, which I had shipped home for later distribution to family and friends. The town of Tillamook sprawls over lush grasslands along the bay and purports to have twice as many cows as people; a prominent sign displays the Tillamook's motto: "Cheese, trees, and ocean breeze."

Continuing north I was drawn to the quaint, seaside hamlet of Cannon Beach. Well-appointed shops, cafés, restaurants, and galleries were neatly arranged along the principal thoroughfare of this artists' colony, which is a popular weekend getaway for Portland residents. In a light drizzle I strolled (for me, a stroll) along the main street before I ventured down the steep pathway to the beach area, a seven-mile swath of packed sand ideal for beachcombing. Dominating the beach is the 235-ft.-tall Haystack Rock, a bullet-shaped monolith that may be the most photographed feature on the entire Oregon coast. Unfortunately, the rain became heavier and curtailed my walk along this expansive and picturesque part of the Oregon coast.

Fig. 25 - "Haystack Rock" monolith on the shores of Cannon Beach, OR

At Cannon Beach I had the unique experience of participating in a tsunami warning drill. When I was walking to my car, an alarm sounded loud and clear. On hearing it, people proceeded to higher ground away from the potentially deadly tsunami waves, and I followed them. Several towns along the Oregon coast employ a similar warning system as an emergency management tool since this region is prone to tsunamis, which can be generated by an earthquake from seismic activity along the fault line off the coast. This drill took place only a few months after a tsunami hit Indonesia causing the deaths of over 100,00 people.

My next stop was the honky-tonk, seafront resort of Seaside, OR, on my itinerary only because of an historical footnote. It was at Seaside that Meriwether Lewis sent several members of his expedition to the beach to collect much needed salt (meat preservative), obtained by boiling off large amounts of sea water for seven continuous days. A replica of the salt cairn used by the men marks the spot on the beach.

The town's main thoroughfare (Broadway) meets the beach at a traffic circle where a large bronze statue of Meriwether Lewis and William Clark is prominently displayed to commemorate their visit. The quantity and variety of commercial establishments in Seaside suggests that during the tourist season large numbers of visitors partake of its carnival-like ambience, reminding me of Old Orchid Beach, ME, or Wildwood, NJ.

My next stop was at one of the most famous sites along the Corps of Discovery's route. It was at Fort Clatsop where the Lewis and Clark expedition spent 106 days in the winter of 1805/1806 before commencing their return journey. This 50-by-50-ft., six-room fort is an authentic representation of their home where they endured rain for all but twelve days. The Visitor Center offers an excellent half-hour video program that depicts the chronology of the expedition and maintains an extensive collection of related artifacts from that period. Unfortunately, in the fall of 2005, the recreated Fort Clatsop was completely destroyed by fire, an accident attributed to a workman's carelessness in using one of the fireplaces.

Fifteen miles further north is Astoria at the tip of Oregon on the Columbia River. Astoria is named for the early fur trader John Jacob Astor, who had become America's wealthiest individual at that time; it is the oldest American city west of the Missouri River. I arrived at the end of the day and checked into a downtown motel before walking to the docks for a tasty wild salmon dinner at a dockside restaurant popular with the locals. The patrons and servers were friendly and engaging, and I enjoyed the camaraderie. I retired for the evening on tax deadline day (April 15th), at what would be my furthest distance from my former home.

I felt blessed to have this opportunity to travel across country unencumbered by finances, schedules, or commitments beyond my present whims. I was pleasantly surprised at my comfort level as a lone traveler, though being able to communicate with family and friends during my journey was gratifying and did much to ease my loneliness. Truthfully, there were moments when a companion would have been welcomed, particularly when I dined at fashionable eateries. But conversations with local patrons and scripting the day's activities in my journal adequately filled most of those moments.

Early the next morning I drove to Astoria Column, atop Coxcomb Hill in a residential section of Astoria. That vantage point offered a commanding view of the confluence of the Columbia River and Pacific Ocean, the coastal plain to the south, and the snowcapped Cascade Range to the East. Unfortunately, a dense layer of fog obscured much of the view; nonetheless it was an impressive sight as it revealed the immense expanse of the Columbia River's mouth, about five miles across. What a sight this must have been for the Corps of Discovery!

Fig. 26 - Confluence of the Columbia River and Pacific Ocean at Astoria, OR

I returned to the waterfront and the Columbia River Maritime Museum. Housed in a large, contemporary building, its exhibits depict the history and geography of the river and the challenges of navigating the treacherous waters at the mouth of the Colombia. The discharge of the river has been compared to a 1,243-mile-long water canon firing, on average, 150 billion gallons of water a day into the ocean surge of the Pacific. The river is the only one in the United States where incoming vessels are required to use the services of a river-bar pilot. Large amounts of cargo are shipped to and from this port and moved upriver to other ports along the inner routes of the Columbia and its tributaries. A large wall map marks the locations of over 2,000 shipwrecks in the waters and at least 700 people have drowned while attempting to navigate the Columbia's entrance.

As the skies finally gave way to sunshine, I drove across the border to Washington state and headed westward through a forested area to an immense, rocky precipice overlooking the entrance to the Columbia River. This is Cape Disappointment, named by the English explorer Captain John Meares, who in 1788 incorrectly interpreted the treacherous sandbars offshore to mean that there was neither a major river nor any other northwest passage here. Despite his misjudgment, Captain Meares, as a member of the Merchant Service, explored much of the coastal northwest, including Alaska, and his discoveries in the region formed the basis upon which Britain originally took title to Oregon and British Columbia.

It was here, on November 7, 1805, 4,000 miles from their start, that the members of Lewis and Clark's expedition finally laid eyes on the Pacific Ocean. From there they moved southward to the aforementioned Fort Clatsop, hoping it would be a more benign environment in which to survive the coming winter.

Fig. 27 - View of Pacific Ocean from farthest point west of Louis and Clark's expedition, Cape Disappointment, WA

At Cape Disappointment The Lewis and Clark Interpretive Center is a comprehensive showcase for their historic journey. In addition to a thirty-two minute highlight film, there is a lecture on the region's early history by a knowledgeable park ranger, as well as an impressive collection of memorabilia, artifacts, and other items relating to the expedition. The chronology of the expedition is dramatically told via a mural along the multiple-level stairwell.

Departing Cape Disappointment I drove eastward along the Washington side of the Columbia River, where several rest areas were highlighted as Lewis and Clark historical sites. I noticed my route was not too far from Mount St. Helen's, the well-known and still active volcano. Although it was late afternoon, the skies were mostly clear, something that more than likely would not be the case the following day. Taking advantage of the good visibility, I drove seventy-five miles on a paved road into the mountains to an overlook where a portion of

Mount St. Helen's could be seen. It was a steep and winding ride with incredible views of the surrounding mountainsides. However, with so many hairpin turns and sharp drop offs, my eyes remained fixed ahead with both hands on the steering wheel. I confess to occasional moments of uneasiness, as the steeply-sloped terrain and absent guard rails were a bit unnerving. The final forty-three miles ended at the uppermost-viewing area and permitted a partial view into the crater of the once 9,700-ft.-high mountain, reduced to 8,300 ft. after blowing its top in 1980.

Due to significant snow accumulations at these elevations, the roads leading to other vistas remained closed. Nonetheless it was impressive to look down into the adjacent valley that once bore the brunt of a superheated mass of volcanic mud flowing down the mountain. In its wake the scarred hillside and newly-formed lakes give testimony to its landscape-altering power. I was the lone visitor; with the final rays of sun giving way to dusk, prudence suggested I negotiate the sinuous, downward return route while it was still light. As darkness set in, a roadside motel on the Columbia River route was a welcome respite.

After a one day break the rain returned as I crossed the Columbia to the Oregon side of the river and visited sites relating to Lewis and Clark's exploration. Each offered its own unique perspective and added to my knowledge of, and appreciation for, the Corps' accomplishments.

The Dalles is a town on the Columbia River where at the time of the expedition the river narrowed, resulting in a restricted flow creating a section of cataract-laced rapids. This slowed-water transport and The Dalles became a popular trading spot. The nearby Lewis and Clark Center had among its exhibits a display that replicated in full scale the thirty tons of cargo inventory with which the Corps of Discovery departed St. Louis at the start of their journey.

Next was a visit to Fort Vancouver along the Columbia River in Vancouver, Washington. I knew nothing of this fort before being told about it a couple of weeks earlier by someone I met en route. It proved to be an especially interesting stop and one with significant history. Fort Vancouver was established as the northwest outpost of the British owned Hudson Bay Company, the most dominant fur trading company of its day. Its strategic location and sympathetic leader played a vital role in the survival of many Americans who were part of the Oregon Trail movement of the mid 1800s.

As explained by a well-versed and enthusiastic guide, the managing director of the fort at that time, John McLaughlin, played a key role. Although forbidden by the company's owners to help settlers establish themselves in the region (as they could become a competitive threat to the business), he nonetheless acted in a most humanitarian manner. McLaughlin saw the dire conditions of many of the settlers who arrived weak, sick, and starving, and he provided them with food and other essential supplies. He justified his generosity to the settlers, while complying with his mandate, by requesting they establish their homesteads well south of Vancouver; of course, many did not. However, his benevolence toward these people so endeared him to Oregonians that in later years he became known as the "Father of Oregon."

Traversing both the Washington and Oregon sides of the Columbia, I was impressed with the river panorama. On the Oregon side the road parallels the river's course from which there are numerous turnoffs leading to impressive waterfalls and cascading tributaries that feed into the river. There was a drenching rain during my visit and waterfalls did little to excite me; whenever I got out of the car, I felt like I was under one!

As I continued toward the eastern end of the Cascades, the rain stopped. The weather became dry and pleasant as I arrived at Hood

River, the gateway city to the Mt. Hood Region and the wind sailing capital of the country. The dry, mild evening made for a pleasant after-dinner walk about town before I retired for the night at an in-town motel.

Realizing my route would be moving southward and away from that of the Lewis and Clark Expedition, I took the opportunity to reflect on the audio tapes of that epic expedition, the first by Ken Burns and the second by Stephen Ambrose. I thought about the extraordinary leadership qualities of Meriwether Lewis and William Clark. Equally impressive were the character and commitment of all the members of the group who met the grueling challenges. That the entire crew of thirty-four persons (save for one member who died of a ruptured appendix at the start of the trip) completed their journey was a tribute to their physical strength and mental toughness, as well as the leadership of Lewis and Clark. Their story is a testimony to man's near limitless capacity for discovery and adventure.

My agenda the following morning included a visit to a couple of local vineyards before driving the loop to majestic Mt. Hood, the symmetrical, cone-shaped mountain, which seems to stand guard over the entire region. The wineries were closed until 11:00 a.m., so I decided to drive the mountain loop. I left the Hood River basin in fifty-degree temperatures under a mostly sunny sky, surrounded by apple and pear orchards in full bloom. Twenty miles and thirty minutes later as I ascended Mt. Hood, clouds engulfed the summit and snow fell at an ever increasing rate atop the already- existing snow cover as my elevation increased.

Of concern to me was the fact that the road was becoming slippery as the snow pack increased with my elevation. As I continued toward Timberline Lodge, six miles ahead, the road steepened considerably and the snowfall was heavier. I noticed the few cars sharing the road with me had either stopped to put on tire chains or turned around. Although I was confident my all-wheel drive SRX could make the final one-mile ascent, my greater concern was that the steepness of the snow-packed road on the return trip might pose a problem. I did not want to have to use snow banks for braking, so I turned around and carefully and successfully retreated to the base of the mountain loop.

Returning to the dry, fragrant Hood River Valley, I stopped at the Pleasant Valley Vineyard, tasted a few of their selections, and purchased a mixed case of their wines for shipment to Connecticut. Since pinot noir had replaced chardonnay as my wine of choice with fish and poultry dishes over the past month (I preferred its fuller body and flavor to that of the usual white wines), a second case of pinot noir was added to the purchase.

My drive south through the high desert region of Oregon passed Warm Springs, a 600,000-acre Indian reservation, home to 3,000 members of the Confederated Tribes of Warm Springs (Wasco, Paiute, and Warm Springs), who were indigenous to the Oregon region. The centerpiece of the reservation was the modern 27,000-sq.-ft. Museum of Warm Springs, with exhibits depicting the history, life, culture, and economy of these Native Americans. It was a particularly educational stop for me since I met one of the reservation's governors; she just happened to stop by to see her son who worked at the museum. I introduced myself to her and we conversed on a variety of topics dealing with the reservation's population and the past treatment of their ancestors by the government.

Logging had provided jobs for tribal members at one time, but its activity ceased with environmental restraints and foreign competition. A casino on the reservation land is a source of modest revenue and the tribe is expected to get state approval to build another one near a major highway, a location of easier access than rural Warm Springs. While these enterprises may fill the tribe's coffers, they would seem to do little to improve the skills and, ultimately, the self worth of their people.

Native American resentment continues to persist over the abuses they were subjected to in earlier times. Written sources (public and private letters and documents) and photographs tell compelling stories of Indian life before, during, and after the settlements were imposed on them by treaty. Children were forced, under threat of imprisonment, to abandon native dress, personal styling, and language so they could better integrate into the "new" American culture! Is it any wonder ill feelings remain among the American Indians over these and other past injustices?

From Warm Springs the road climbs up a steep canyon, then plateaus at Madras, the county seat of Jefferson County and once known as the "mint capital of the world." Currently, mint production trails several vegetable crops and flowers commercially grown in the area and tourism has quietly become an economic mainstay for Madras. The Deschutes River has carved its way through the steep canyons and outdoor recreation opportunities abound. Rock hounding, fishing, hunting, rafting, and boating are all popular activities.

Though temperatures overnight were expected to drop below freezing, I headed to nearby Cove Palisades State Park, situated within the volcanic canyons of the region, to pitch my tent. Before retiring that night, I took an hour or so walk along the upper canyon trail. The steep canyon walls bounded the expansive Deschutes River and reservoir, the latter a popular summer recreation area as evidenced by numerous boat launches and docks. It has the apparent capacity to accommodate a small naval force. The park was deserted except for the caretakers. There's usually one such site in a campground where the occupants, mostly retired individuals or couples, stay for extended periods. Their camping fee is minimal since they look after the grounds and monitor the activities within. During the course of my campground stays I met several such people, and their personalities varied as much as their trailer varieties. Clearly some enjoyed meeting new people and sharing their experiences and knowledge of the region. Others seemed more introverted, preferring the quietness of these nature retreats with little to say besides checking that the site fees were paid (for after-hour or off- season visitors).

For reasons I didn't understand, I felt lonely; not alone but lonely. It was one of the few times during my travels that such a feeling came over me. I missed the companionship of someone, maybe anyone. Why at this particular time? It may have been that there was little going on to stimulate my interest, or that I wanted to share my latest experiences with somebody.

A bit dejected, I climbed into my sleeping bag, brought my journal up to date, and was asleep within the hour. As predicted, the temperature was in the upper twenties at sunrise, and a hot shower in the nearby bath facility was a godsend. After breaking camp I drove south, stopping outside Bend for a half-day visit to the High Desert Museum. This extensive facility highlighted the flora and fauna of the high desert region with live specimens of both on display. Several varieties of native birds including a golden eagle and other birds of prey were housed in screened areas throughout the museum's grounds. There were interpretative talks, displays, and artifacts relating to the Indian tribes of this region that told the story of their plight during the past two hundred years.

A highlight was the guided tour of the Oregon Trail exhibits by a competent and enthusiastic member of the museum's staff. This mass migration westward, which began in the 1840s, and opened up the western part of the United States to expansion, was dramatically and poignantly recreated with a series of life-size dioramas portraying events as they would have occurred along that journey. In chronological order the scenes depicted the elements of such a journey that would be part of a "typical" day and included habits of dress, eating, and sleeping, along with the settlers dealing with the challenges of the trip: extreme weather and harsh conditions, equipment breakdowns, Indian attacks, sickness, and death.

The Oregon Trail did not follow the Lewis and Clark route; the latter would not have permitted wagons to cross the mountains. It was John Steward, a member of John Jacob Astor's Fur Trading Company, who in 1808 helped establish the Astor Trading Company and trail blazed the principal route through a twelve-mile pass in the Rockies. The thirty-year interval between the discovery of that route and its practical use was because John Jacob Astor would not permit his employees to reveal it; Astor feared potential competitors moving west. One could reasonably surmise his immense wealth was not a product of inattention to detail.

From the storied history of the past to the natural beauty of the present, I continued south into the Umpqua National Forest and Crater Lake National Park. Crater Lake is set in a dormant volcano, Mt. Mazama, which is part of the same volcanic chain as Mt. St. Helens. Its caldera has accumulated sufficient water over the centuries to make Crater Lake, at 1,900 feet, the deepest lake in the United States. I was disappointed to see that the higher elevations had substantial snow cover, and many roads and hiking trails were closed. I had to reroute around the lake, since the entry road from my northerly direction remained closed. With a subfreezing night forecasted, I found lodging in the tiny, nearby hamlet of Prospect. The inn at the edge of town was the stately *Prospect Historical Hotel*, a distinguished home during the latter part of the 19th century. It's owner, A.H. Boothby, hosted a gilded list of overnight guests, including Teddy Roosevelt, Herbert Hoover, and authors Zane Grey and Jack London, among others. *Maybe some of their literary genius will rub off on me!*

I woke to sunny blue skies reminiscent of my trek through the southwest and learned from the innkeeper of the excellent hiking trails in the area leading to several scenic waterfalls and cataracts along the Rogue River, which bisects this hamlet. I availed myself of this opportunity; it had been a while since my last hikes because of the poor trail conditions in the snowy forests of the higher elevations.

I followed my hour-and-a-half hike with a drive to the rim of Crater Lake along the only open road leading to its 7,000-ft. summit. The thirty-three mile road that actually rims the crater was buried under eight feet of snow and not expected to open before the end of June; all that snow despite the fact that this year's snowfall was below the seasonal average! As is the case with many parts of the Sierras, Cascades, and Rockies, snow accumulations render large portions of these magnificent landscapes closed to road vehicles until the end of June, or even in some cases, July. Then visitors arrive en mass. I think the optimum time to visit is early autumn, but then there is not nearly enough time to see more than two or three of these parks before early winter snow arrives.

Fig. 28 - Snow at 7,000 feet packs the rim road at Crater Lake National Park, OR

Descending to warmer elevations, I continued to the recreational hub of the Rogue River and Shady Cove. The outdoor activities in this region are centered on the river made famous by its salmon and steelhead runs. This was the same river I fished for Chinook salmon at Gold Beach along the Oregon coast a few weeks before. The fish of choice would now be steelhead trout since the salmon are several weeks away from this portion of the river. I made arrangements with a local guide for the following morning.

That afternoon I toured the Cole River Hatchery, reportedly the largest in Oregon and among the largest in the western United States. It was an interesting visit made more memorable because I met and conversed with a grizzled veteran of these waters who seemed to have answers to all the fish-related questions I could throw his way. Don had fished this region for decades and we conversed as he hand-rolled a cigarette while sitting behind the wheel of his twenty-year-old van. Judging from the contents of his van, including a cot in the rear, I think it may serve as his home or at least a second one. Come to think of it, somewhat similar to my own situation!

The weather had been very pleasant. There was a scenic municipal campground on the Rogue River outside of Shady Cove where I pitched my tent, dined on the usual camp fare, and retired to my sleeping bag. I expected nighttime temperatures to remain above freezing; the good news was that it did, the bad news was that my new air mattress deflated during the night, leaving me awake for several hours.

At 8:00 my guide Bob arrived at my campsite with his boat and fishing gear. We headed up river to put in with his 17-ft., flat-bottom aluminum boat. The fishing technique we used is called "side drifting": Bob directed the boat through the swift currents of the shallow waters with his oars, while I cast the salmon roe bait upstream on either side of the boat as instructed. The hope was that it would drift in front of or near to a steelhead that would be sufficiently interested or annoyed to attack it.

The day warmed nicely under a bright blue sunny sky; the waters were extraordinarily clear and the tree-lined bank of the Rogue River made an inspirational and attractive scene. This is a rather wordy way of saying that while no fish were landed, the experience was exhilarating and fun. The question I'm inevitably asked by friends and family alike is: "Did you catch any fish?" My candid answer always is: *That question is irrelevant. It has no meaning because fishing is not about catching fish. It is about the totality of the experience and, in that sense, I was extraordinarily successful.* I don't know what kind of mileage I will ultimately get from that statement, but I will certainly continue to use it.

I read about a small town Jacksonville just south of Shady Cove and asked Bob, who was born and raised in this area, about it. He recommended I go there; it was one of the West's first gold/silver mining towns. I arrived there by late afternoon and after inquiring at the visitor's bureau, I selected the picturesque *Magnolia Inn B&B* for my evening stay. My walk around the fully-restored historical section of the town was not especially stimulating, but the warm, sunny day was a welcome change from my last few days in the wilderness of the parks. A dinner of fresh Pacific salmon at the historical *Jacksonville Inn* was an apt reward for the outdoor rigors of the last several days. I especially enjoyed my conversation with Mary, the bartender, a native of the area with a passion for the outdoors, especially fly fishing. Interestingly, she learned her fishing skills from Bob, my guide of the previous day, on the same river where I had been unsuccessful.

The next morning I took a walk to see numerous historic buildings in the downtown area; they now housed a variety of commercial, professional, and retail businesses and offered little of interest to me. From there it was a moderately strenuous uphill walk to the cemetery where many of the region's notable citizens were interred, including Peter Britt and his family. Peter, to quote a local commentary, "was one of Jacksonville's best known and most respected pioneers. He is remembered today for the pictures he took, the plants he grew, and now the music festival that bears his name."

Peter Britt was an extraordinary man of vision and accomplishment. Arriving in Jacksonville at the start of the Gold Rush, he was a prospector and mule packer before finding his first love, photography. He continued to capture on film the people and landscapes of southern Oregon for nearly fifty years. He also found time to pursue his interests in horticulture, wine making, beekeeping, and meteorology. His financial acumen served him well, and when he died at the age of eighty-six in 1905, Peter Britt was one of the wealthiest, best known, and most respected men in Oregon.

Leaving Jacksonville for a short ride on Interstate 5, I was rewarded with broad views of Mt. Shasta, California's 14,000-ft. jewel, which dominated the landscape. I exited onto a secondary road in the direction of Lassen Volcano National Park, suspecting the remaining snow pack would keep the park closed for at least another month. Meanwhile, I was pleasantly surprised to come upon the hamlet of McCloud, nestled on the southern slope of Mt. Shasta. It is an old mill town named for Alexander McCloud, an employee of the early fur trading empire, Hudson Bay Company. It continued to be a company-owned town into the 20th century and a fact that has created some governmental and management issues within the township. A few well-connected residents allegedly exert disproportionate leverage on the outcome of town matters. I spoke with a couple of local citizens about the issue, including one retail shop owner who says the rights to the region's largest aquifer of superb quality spring drinking water had been assigned to a major corporation, Nestles, for a fraction of its value. The complaints center on the lack of a democratic process in the decision and a feeling among the locals that the powers to be "sold out" to big business for a quick influx of revenue. The matter is currently being contested by an activist group of townspeople who are hoping to have the courts overturn the earlier decision.

Inquiring at the local U.S. Forestry Center, I was directed to an area twelve miles away where a ten-mile hike along a cascading, waterfall-laden stream promised to be rewarding. Driving along a rough gravel road for several miles, seemingly removed from civilization, I finally arrived at the trailhead. There was a large van in the parking area, which suggested to me I would not be alone -- a measure of comfort since I was hiking in a remote area. It was a delightful walk, paralleling the hyperactive stream along the entire route in a thickly treed forest. Was I ever surprised four miles into the hike when I encountered a group of eight ladies ahead of me on the same trail. They were from nearby Redding, and every so often they venture outdoors as a group for a day of exercise and camaraderie. They were certainly a social bunch not lacking for conversation. We exchanged a couple of "trail tales" and they enjoyed my story of the bear visit I had in Sequoia National Park. I then continued ahead of them after we said our goodbyes, eventually returning to the trailhead and my car.

I remained overnight in McCloud and dined at the *McCloud Inn*, a mansion from the late 1800s. I was rewarded with an exceptional rib eye steak and equally good vegetable and other accompaniments, all of which placed this meal well up my top ten list of favorite dining experiences.

Rain the next morning discouraged me from hiking in the McCloud Falls area that, as I noted from photographs, would have been an interesting and scenic hike. As I neared Lassen Volcanic National Park, the rain subsided, which was a relief because at the higher elevation, the precipitation would have been snow. Still, I could go only ten miles to the first Visitor Center where I viewed a vast area of volcanic debris and had a reasonable look at 10,000-ft. Mt. Lassen. A park ranger said there was fifteen feet of snow packed on the main road around the rim of the crater. Snow removal had just begun during that third week of April. The snow is not removed by plowing, which would be impossible given how tightly packed it gets. Instead, an auger is attached to a bulldozer-like vehicle, which grinds into the snow. This action breaks down the snow pack, and mechanized shovels and trucks then remove it at the rate of a quarter-mile of road per day. Therefore, the expected time for a fully-opened road would be six weeks... a June opening.

From Lassen National Park a two-hour drive brought me to the small town of Susanville, CA, where the local theater featured *"Fever Pitch,"*, the movie about the Boston Red Sox' World-Series-winning year of 2004. After a mid-afternoon motel check-in, I enjoyed a mental change of pace at the movies. Go Red Sox!!!!

On a dreary Sunday morning I left Susanville after attending mass and meandered south on Route 89 around Lake Tahoe's western side. The two-hour ride took me past sparsely-settled villages with ranches and farms scattered among the cradle of the surrounding mountains. Upon reaching the lake, I formed some contradictory impressions. Unquestionably, the Lake Tahoe region is a beautiful sight with alpine peaks and lush evergreen forests surrounding the deep blue waters of the lake: a photographer's paradise. Yet I was disappointed by the unattractiveness of my immediate surroundings. Large mounds of snow were piled all around -- dark, dirty snow discolored by a continual flow of traffic. Furthermore, the roadside seemed littered with restaurants, motels, coffee shops, and a myriad of gift and related tourist stores.

In all fairness to Lake Tahoe, because I had been traveling among our country's greatest natural wonders and with minimal human intrusion, my perspective may have been prejudiced. My guess was that in the less commercial, upper portions of Tahoe such as Incline Village, dotted with the enclaves of the mega rich, it would be more attractive. Thankfully, this proved to be the case.

I looked forward to hiking and otherwise exploring the Tahoe region with my friend Cheryl, who would be arriving in a couple of days. In the interim I continued eastward past South Tahoe to Carson City, the capital city of Nevada where I found lodging at a downtown motel. The city's commercial and retail businesses, governmental facilities, and casinos were concentrated along a single main street, all within reasonable walking distance of each other. The next morning I walked to the Nevada Historical Museum about a mile from my motel, past government buildings and a few garish casinos. The museum was housed in the building that formerly served as a U.S. Mint in the late 19th century. In addition to an interesting collection of historical artifacts depicting the significance of Carson City's mining operation in an earlier era, there were extensive wall murals that chronicled the geological activity in this region, which accounted for the formation of the Great Basin, Nevada's principal topological feature. The region is rich in mineral deposits and fossil beds, and I especially appreciated the mineral and paleontology exhibits.

Nearby the famous Comstock Lode was discovered in 1859, one of the richest strikes in history. Its gold and silver production brought riches to many and gave birth to Virginia City. The museum offered a walk through a full-scale model of a hard rock mine and gave me a sense of what it was like to be a miner in those times.

Not having any interest in the nearby casinos, I left Carson City for Reno via Virginia City, over and around mountains containing miles of hairpin turns overlooking the rugged hills and valley below. Portions of the drive went past abandoned mines and mineral processing works now rusting away along the roadside. I continued through Virginia City without stopping, noting that while it was clearly a tacky tourist trap, it managed to retain a certain mystique.

In Reno my only interest, other than meeting up with Cheryl, was to visit Bill Harrah's Antique Auto Museum, perhaps the most valuable collection of vintage automobiles anywhere. A two-hour guided tour provided fascinating background stories of various cars and was directed by an extremely knowledgeable, affable gentleman. On display was the automobile which won the first around-the-world race from New York City to Paris via the Pacific route. Also included were many items that accompanied its crew during their 1908 epic achievement. The trophy, alleged to be the largest ever made and presented to the winner of a sporting event, was on display as well. It is in the shape of a globe mounted onto a pedestal and weighs 1,600 lbs.

With Cheryl due to arrive that evening, I used the daytime hours to play a round of golf at the Wolf Run Golf Course in Reno. My playing partners were a father and son pair; the former had retired to Reno from Southern California and his son was in the construction business in the Reno area. Judging by the endless cluster of new homes surrounding the course and conversations with Bill's son, Richard, the home building boom was in full force.

Later that evening, Cheryl arrived in Reno and the next morning, a cold, dreary one, we drove to Lake Tahoe via Virginia City. At the peak of the gold and silver finds during the latter part of the 19th century, Virginia City was the largest settlement between San Francisco and Chicago. In its mining aftermath, and with the help of the TV series *Bonanza*, it is now a popular tourist stop with the entire trappings one would expect, i.e. restaurants, bars, souvenir shops, stores of all sorts, and, of course, gaming machines en mass.

Despite the commercialism of Virginia City, its history made for an interesting trolley tour. Many of the buildings and other features of the original city remain to this day, and its past was recounted in detail by an animated and entertaining guide. A downtown coffee shop served, by Cheryl's estimate, the worst cup of cappuccino she'd ever had, but since I don't drink those overpriced coffee concoctions, I couldn't validate her assessment.

Our route out of Virginia City took us through abandoned mining towns like Silver City, where the remnants of mining operations remained scattered along the gouged hillsides from which the precious metals were extracted. Mounds of tailings serve as testimony to the earlier glory days when so much wealth was created from the metallic bounty of the mountains.

With temperatures in the thirties at the high elevations of Lake Tahoe, we drove along the southerly portion, making occasional stops at panoramic vistas. With dark, cloudy skies and windy conditions, Cheryl's enthusiasm for seeing the lake from outside the car was rather muted and she repeatedly commented about not having brought the right clothing for this trip. Translation: *I need my winter clothing.*

We checked into the Marriott Grand Hotel, centrally located on the California side within the resort community of South Lake Tahoe. A gondola to the top of the ski area was adjacent to the hotel, which itself is an anchor to the upscale shopping village surrounding it. Unless one's interest is in gambling (Harrah's and Caesars' casinos dominate the border town of Stateline, Nevada), the Grand Marriott is the preferred premier hotel in the southern Tahoe area. Our first dinner in Tahoe was at *The Chart House* and it was memorable: excellent food, nice ambiance, and views of the lake from our hillside location.

With a questionable weather forecast, we planned a morning drive west toward Sacramento in search of the sun and warmth obviously missing thus far at the higher elevations of Tahoe. An hour from Tahoe we turned off at Plymouth into the Shenandoah Valley. There had to be over twenty vineyards within a twenty-five mile radius. In contrast to the sprawling estates of the Napa vineyards, most of these were of modest proportions, though attractive in their own right. The manicured vineyards and lovely hillsides with flowers of all colors adorning their slopes made for a wonderfully relaxed and romantic sojourn through the region. We made several stops at selected wineries; we toured their properties, enjoyed our wine tasting, and purchased some of our favorite choices for consumption back home.

We were charmed by the attractiveness of the region, made especially appealing by sunny skies and temperatures in the upper sixties. Maybe Cheryl didn't need her winter attire after all! A mountain lion dashed across the road late in the afternoon and added a bit of excitement to a very rewarding day.

Back at Lake Tahoe the weather was much improved and was ideal for the following day's ride around the lake. A side trip to Squaw Valley, site of the 1960 Winter Olympics and Olympic village was fun, especially the aerial tram ride to the summit of the mountain. At the top were a swimming pool, jacuzzi, restaurants and cocktail lounge, and the Olympic museum, which displayed photos and memorabilia from the

1960 Olympics. Though the ski season was winding down, several skiers and snowboarders were visible on the slopes.

After a poolside lunch at 11,000 feet, we returned to Olympic Village for a little window shopping before resuming our drive north around upper Tahoe to Incline Village, the part-time retreat for the mega rich where lakeside home prices may reach $30 million. Frankly, I was not impressed with what one gets for $10 million on the lake. In fact, as I noted in correspondence to a friend back home, home values here and at other high profile areas that I had seen on my trip, suggest it will not be all that long before Watch Hill will see prices for premier homes in the $20 million price range; it is just too beautiful and special a place not to have home values comparable to those of the premier real estate enclaves of our country. Maybe I was prophetic, but the following year a residential property in Watch Hill sold for $17 million!

Our good-weather fortunes continued and we began the next day with a couple of hikes, including one a mile long down a very steep pathway to a beachfront mansion on the shore of Emerald Bay. It was built by a Norwegian heiress and remains closed and boarded up today.

After a second modest hike, Cheryl and I opted for a two-hour ferry ride on the lake to and from Emerald Bay. It was a relaxing ride on the paddle- driven boat, and we enjoyed the pleasant weather and each other's company. It was our last night in Tahoe and we returned to *The Chart House* for our farewell dinner and recollections of a wonderful time.

On Sunday, May 1st, Cheryl and I left Lake Tahoe for the Reno airport and our return flight to Connecticut. The day also marked the 13th birthday of my grandson Zachary as well as the 63rd of his grandfather, now a firmly- entrenched senior citizen!

LEG FOUR: EASTWARD BOUND

After celebrating family birthdays, including mine, Zach's, his mom's (my daughter Cher) and Mother's Day, I returned to Reno to rejoin my well- rested Caddy SRX. There began the final leg of my journey, starting with an eastward drive through Nevada along what is known as the "loneliest road in America" (Route 50). However, until one gets past Fallon, the road seems more commercial than lonely. With the creation of the Lahontan Reservoir from the Carson River, Fallon's agriculture has thrived. Alfalfa, onions, garlic, and prized cantaloupes are the agricultural mainstays of this area; their fields ring this oasis city within Nevada's Great Desert Basin. Fallon is a thriving community of 8,000 residents supported by agriculture and the nearby Naval Air Station, an important training center for the Navy's elite (Top Gun) fighter pilots.

From here the road wore its "loneliest road" label accurately as traffic and buildings of any kind thinned out rapidly. My first stop was at Grimes' Point, where a self-guided trail led to hundreds of petroglyphs etched into the basalt boulders strewn along the pathways. These eight-centuries old carvings have yet to be deciphered but suggest a theme describing activities of the time.

Nearby is a formation known as Hidden Cave, used as a dumping site until someone noticed artifacts from ancient people entombed there.

Since then significant archaeological remains have been unearthed. The area is now closed to visitors, but it can be toured with advance reservations on selected days. Nowhere was the confluence of the old and new more apparent than here; across the vast plain to my east was the site of the Naval Air Station, where many of our country's newest and fastest jets are put through their paces. While I hiked among ancient remains, 21st-century Navy jets screeched in the skies above me.

Further east I came upon Sand Mountain, an immense sand dune whose profile was as well defined as that of a Swiss mountain. The two-mile-long formation abruptly rose to six hundred feet and was a magnet for recreational dirt bikers and ATVers, who drove up and down the steep slopes. It was Saturday and I suspected the throngs of campers along the base of the dune and the multitude of bikers represented a busy weekend for the park staff of just one person. There were few biking regulations in effect, and therefore not many rules to enforce, which was testimony to minimal government interference at this national recreation site.

Fig. 29 - Campers with ATVs enjoying the challenges of 600-ft.-high Sand Mountain, NV

In the same area were the remnants of a Pony Express relay station. This was the route used by the U.S. Postal Service during its runs from St. Joseph, MO, to Sacramento, CA, from 1860 to 1861. All that remains of the station are crumbled stone walls that define the rooms as well as the adjacent horse corral. I sat in the open corner of one section and imagined what it was like almost one-hundred-fifty years ago. What a lonely outpost it must have been!

From here I turned off Route 50 onto State Route 361 for a fifty-mile side trip to the Berlin-Ichthyosaur State Park, which includes the hundred-year- old ghost town of Berlin, as well as a 225-million-year-old marine fossil quarry. Apropos the "loneliest road in America": this route and S.R. 844 with its paved and dirt roads make Route 50 seem like the Connecticut Turnpike. Free ranges were on both sides of the road and occasional wayward cattle along the roadside necessitated *slowing* to 80 mph. With no car or truck sightings; the absence of power lines, homes, or other man-made structures; and zero phone signal; if my car broke down I'd have become as fossilized as those creatures I was so anxious to see in Berlin!

Fortunately no such mishaps occurred, and I finally arrived at the terminus of a long and dusty dirt road marking the entrance to the state park. The Visitor Center is housed in one of the buildings in the ghost town of Berlin. I set up my tent in the camping area, where I was surprised to find several sites occupied. It was a weekend, but where did these people come from? They were certainly willing to rough it since the campground lacked water, electricity, or sewage facilities; the only power in Berlin was supplied by a generator.

As there was a scheduled tour of the fossil site that afternoon, I immediately proceeded there. As I was the only visitor, I had a personalized tour of the area. The fossil beds are protected by a large timber-supported metal enclosure and contained several in-situ specimens of Ichthyosaurs, prehistoric marine reptiles whose length reached as much as fifty-four feet. One of the fossils was a nearly complete skeleton of the animal that remained just as it was found. Upon inquiring why the fossilized skeletons were not removed from their rock encasement, I was told scientists believed more could be learned by observations of the remains in their final positions. Also, the bedrock immediately surrounding the fossils was a hard, granite-like stone likely to make removing the skeletal remains intact a risky undertaking.

My tour concluded by midday and I decided to hike to the Richmond Mine, an abandoned silver mine three miles from the fossil site and over the adjacent hills through a dense woodland. Rattlesnakes were active in the area, so my main focus was watching where I was stepping. The hike proceeded without incident; however, with an elevation of 7,000 feet and perhaps because I had been back home for several days and gotten out of my hiking mode, it was a strenuous trek.

After returning to camp I took a seven-mile drive over a well-tracked dirt road to another abandoned mining town, Iona, population under fifty. Beer, soft drinks, and little else could be bought at the saloon, the only public place in the generator-powered town. After my strenuous hike, a cold Corona (dollar a bottle) tasted as good as one would at the 19th hole after walking a round of golf on a mid-summer day in Stonington. I returned to camp for my version of a gourmet camp dinner: salmon mousse, crackers, sardines, an apple, and Cheryl's delicious, home-baked brownies. After dinner I wanted to journal the day's activity, but I was too tired; by 8:30 I had climbed into my sleeping bag and was fast asleep, not awakening until 3:00 a.m.

By sunrise I was out and about under sunny blue skies and mild temperatures. I planned to tour Berlin's Diane Mine, a hard-rock gold and silver mine. Since the mine tour did not start for several hours, I used the time to update my journal, followed by a walk around the dozen or so buildings that remained in Berlin. These were restored only to the extent necessary to preserve their character and structural integrity.

It was a short walk to the mine, which I toured with four other visitors, all of us outfitted with lanterns and hard hats as we carefully walked through the 650-ft. abandoned tunnel. We followed the route through the mine, had the procedures described, and saw the tools used to extract the gold and silver ores. Many of the tools and supplies used by the miners were left behind as if they were to return the next day!

Instead of retracing my route back to Route 50, I decided to take a shortcut via Rural Route 21, a hard-packed dirt road to Austin, another former-mining town struggling to survive. I stopped there only long enough for a quick lunch and continued to the Hickison Petroglyph

Recreation Area. A short, walking trail looped through the vegetation of pinon pines, juniper, sagebrush, and other less familiar vegetation. I passed dozens of sandstone boulders adorned with ancient figures, some of which date to 10,000 B.C. Considering the close proximity of the petrographs to the trail, I was surprised they remained graffiti-free.

The road from Austin to Eureka has to be the loneliest, straightest, seventy-five mile stretch of pavement anywhere. Were it not for the occasional cattle grazing on the free range all about me, I would have comfortably covered the distance at 120 mph. But alas, the risk of being confronted on the road by a quarter ton steer kept me under 90 mph and I arrived at Eureka an hour later. Located in the middle of Nevada's Great Basin, Eureka continues to thrive with numerous operating gold mines. Though I thought of spending the night there, the several hours of daylight remaining enabled me to continue another eighty miles to the former mining town of Ely. Unlike previous towns whose prosperity waxed and waned with gold and silver, Ely's mining prosperity came from the extraction of copper from the mineral-rich adjacent mountains. Here, open pit mining operations continued until the 1980s. Today huge mounds of tailings share the landscape with the equally barren, mountainous terrain of the Great Basin.

I spent the night at the landmark *Midtown Hotel*, complete with a gambling casino, pool tables, bars, and a restaurant. Several reasonably-priced rooms were on the second level; they were hardly luxury caliber, but more than sufficient for my needs: clean room with a hot shower and bed. After a barely edible steak dinner in the hotel's restaurant and quickly parting with twenty dollars in a slot machine, I retired for the evening. In the morning I went to the Nevada North Railway Museum, which occupies the former site of an open pit copper mining operation. Kennecott Inc. abruptly shut down the entire operation in the early 1980s leaving everything behind. The town of Ely renovated the facility making it a tourist draw for the region. The museum complex included a string of shops along the railroad tracks as well as several operating steam and diesel trains used for tours of the area. I spoke with a few of the shopkeepers, and it was refreshing to hear them share their enthusiasm for a successful rebirth of Ely.

The drive northward on Route 93 to Twin Falls, ID, could compete with Route 50 as the loneliest road in America. I passed expansive fields of sagebrush extending to a horizon limited only by the snowcapped Ruby Mountains to the west, otherwise known as the Nevada Alps. Just prior to entering Idaho, I stopped for lunch along the rainy route (rain in Nevada?) at Jackpot, a town consisting of a few casinos and little else. Of note to geological buffs: Jackpot is situated on the Columbia plateau where it occupies the only sliver of land in Nevada that is not part of the two major deserts that comprise the entire state, i.e. The Great Basin and the Mojave.

If Nevada is the most desolate of our contiguous forty-eight states, then in the preceding three days I believe I traversed the most desolate parts of this most desolate state. It will remain a treasured memory as I came to understand, appreciate, and enjoy the geology, geography, and history of the Great Basin region. The many abandoned mines, together with the towns built around them, tell compelling stories of the rise and fall of the fortunes of the early residents of the region. Although driving this vast, barren area made me apprehensive as a solitary traveler, the stark beauty of the mountains and the seemingly endless sea of tumbleweed and scattered heads of cattle dominated my psyche. The lengthy, uninterrupted drive north was an especially meditative period during which I enjoyed listening to a compact disc of C.S. Lewis' *Mere Christianity*.

Fig. 30 - Loneliest of the lonely roads, somewhere in Nevada's Great Basin

Crossing into Idaho brought about a notable change in the landscape, where grassy meadows replaced the flat sagebrush terrain. Gently rolling hills now highlighted the horizon previously dominated by snowcapped mountains. I arrived in Twin Falls, located on the Snake River near to where Evel Knievel failed in his attempt to jump his motorcycle across the river's breadth in 1974. The city is located in the heart of a very productive region of irrigated croplands extending over one-half million acres throughout southern Idaho. I checked into a motel after stopping by the local Visitor Center to accumulate maps and travel brochures to help plan my itinerary over the next couple of days. A local steakhouse *Jakes* brought a satisfying conclusion to a long day of travel with a sumptuous Omaha filet of beef; this was definitely a top-ten meal!

Awakening on a cool, clear, sunny morning, I drove a few miles to the Shoshone Falls in Dierkes Lake and took a scenic 3 ½-mile walk around the lake, framed by the canyon walls of the Snake River ecosystem. I then continued towards Sun Valley, one of the most famous destination ski resorts in the country. I stopped along the way in Hailey which with Ketchum (it's more glitzy and traffic snarled sister city just a few miles north) is the epicenter of Sun Valley. I stopped only long enough for a much overpriced breakfast at Shorty's Diner (owned by Hollywood starlet Demi Moore).

My next destination was the Craters-of-the-Moon National Monument, a desolate area of volcanic lava fields stretching over 60,000 acres. It was once described by Washington Irving as a place "where nothing meets the eye but a desolate and awful waste, where no trees grow, where no grass grows, nor water runs, and where nothing is to be seen but lava." Though very windy, the bright sunny day and temperatures in the fifties afforded excellent hiking conditions. With many turnouts along the park route I hiked at several sites among the lava-formed topography. The concluding trails were most interesting as they led to several subsurface lava tubes or caves that I wandered through, flashlight in hand, for several hundred feet. By the time I departed the park, I had done a few hours of aggressive hiking.

Leaving Craters-of-the-Moon by late afternoon, I drove through Idaho Falls to Jackson, WY. The beauty of the landscape was stunning, and it was made even more so by the final rays of the setting sun. Arriving in Jackson Hole, I checked into a downtown hotel and enjoyed a delicious rib eye steak at the *Cowboy Steak House*, which brought to an end a full day of hiking and driving. This was my first three-hundred-mile-driving day, which I undertook only because of the longer daylight hours and wonderful scenery from Idaho Falls to Jackson.

Awakening to a cold, overcast day, I delayed my short ride out of Jackson to Grand Teton National Park, hoping to see clearing skies. In the interim I opted for a walk around town and window shopped at an endless array of gift shops, galleries, and the usual run of souvenir stores as well as several national clothing chains. I can only imagine what the tourist season must be like here to support this huge conglomeration of retail stores and restaurants.

Before leaving town I passed a Smith Barney brokerage office and thought I'd have some "fun" with my good friend Jack. Yes, the same passionate golfer who was responsible for my Bandon Dunes foray is also my valued Smith Barney financial advisor and broker. At this time he would just be arriving at his Hartford, CT, office. I introduced myself to the affable manager of the one-man office and after appropriate validations and disclaimers he agreed to go along with my ploy, but only to the extent of placing the call on my behalf to Jack indicating he was calling from the firm's Jackson Hole office. After this he handed the phone to me.

I greeted Jack with an excited, yet concerned tone (remember, I was chosen Class Dramatist of my high school class). We exchanged pleasantries before I informed him that I'd fallen in love with the area and would be purchasing a dream home here. Jack was well aware that I was homeless at this point, so his measured response was congratulatory -- that is, until I asked him what's involved in transferring all the assets of my investment accounts to the Jackson office? I thought the line went dead! After a pause, and before any response, I said: "Jack, relax, it's just my version of western humor!" And our professional relationship continues to this day.

It was now on to the national park to pitch my tent at a campsite along Jenny Lake at the base of the Teton Range and near a trailhead that leads to a six- mile hike around the lake. With improving weather and after a quick lunch at my campsite, I commenced my walk about the lake, which included stops at Hidden Falls and Inspiration Point. It was an invigorating hike but I thought it would never end; six miles never seemed so long to me.

Instead of returning to my site I traveled the park's main road to capture the full views of the majestic profile of the Teton Mountains. In the absence of foothills, the snowcapped, granite pinnacles rise abruptly through steep conifer forests to over 7,000 feet. Grand Teton Mountain at 13,770-ft. high is the most dominant of all; its jagged, well-defined peak highlights the horizon. Along my route I noticed the park's restaurant was open and I treated myself to a cheese buffalo burger, which proved to be quite good. I couldn't tell the difference from its cousin, the beef burger.

During dinner I met a lodge employee who had lived in Narragansett, RI, and arrived in Wyoming after retiring from Electric Boat in Groton, CT. Talk about a small world!

I broke camp during an intermittent rain the following morning and started out at 6 o'clock to view the wildlife activity (buffalo and elk) along the grassland route leading to Yellowstone National Park, forty miles north.

Though there were no cloudless skies during my stay, the cloud-interrupted profile of the mountain range was a superlative vista to behold. To best appreciate the spectacle of the Tetons, the park should be entered from the north (Yellowstone's direction) where the main road coming into the park affords a view of the Snake River in the foreground with the Teton Range as a magnificent backdrop. These are young mountains, still growing, in which the softer sedimentary rocks have been eroded leaving a hard granite matrix. The resulting jagged and irregular outline dominates the skyline. Ansel Adams famously captured on film this remarkable landscape formed by the Tetons and the Snake River in the foreground.

I entered Yellowstone from the southwestern section of this 2.2-million-acre geological menagerie, the world's first national park, established in 1872. Initially I found myself surrounded by the scarred landscape resulting from the momentous 1988 fires. Almost one-third of the park's acreage was affected, but as environmentalists later learned, the ecology of the region and its flora and fauna were impacted in a positive way and healthy balances among the plant and animal species were reestablished. The charred acreage all about offered no clues to the magnificent landscape and adventures that lay ahead for me at Yellowstone.

My initial stop was at the venerable *Old Faithful Lodge* to secure a room for the evening. The remaining snow cover in this region of the park, together with cold temperatures, discouraged me from camping. Most of the campgrounds were closed anyway because of the activities of Yellowstone's large grizzly bear population. Not long awakened from their winter hibernation, the bears were hungry and the sows were foraging about with their cubs. Consequently, many hiking trails were also closed with the notice "No Trespassing - Bear Closure."

It was May 15th but the park's main roads had been opened to visitors for only a week as the winter season lingered. I looked forward to seeing as much of the scenery and wildlife as possible. It was early morning and with my cabin not ready I walked over to the geyser area where "Old Faithful" is situated. At the strong recommendation of a park ranger, I also stopped by the camp store and purchased bear bells that are attached to the hiker's belt or backpack and are supposed to make enough noise to alert a bear to one's presence. In theory, the bear's propensity is to avoid humans and the noise sends it scurrying away. I also bought a canister of pepper spray, one of the more popular items for sale.

Grizzlies can appear anywhere and as a lone hiker I had to be very cautious. I wasn't sure what comfort could be expected from the bear spray, since it is effective only at twenty feet or closer. Bears have a habit of false charging and the instructions were not to spray the bear unless the charge is real. Now think about that for a moment! The spray is effective from within twenty feet, but it shouldn't be used until the bear's intent is clear. This raises important questions: at what distance does one determine a charging bear is not just bluffing? How fast is the charge? Or put another way, how many nano seconds does one have to unleash a spray? And finally, even if I manage to answer questions one and two correctly, how soon will a bear alter its charge after being sprayed? There could be some interesting days ahead.

My initial Yellowstone hike was without incident. I enjoyed walking the six- mile loop that encircled Old Faithful Geyser from above. Bison and their calves were scattered along the trail seemingly oblivious to my presence. Approaching these apparently tame, yet wild small herds (representative of their ancestors who once numbered in the tens of millions across the plains) was both an unnerving and a tranquil experience. From the summit of an adjacent hilltop, I watched the predicted eruption of Yellowstone's legendary "Old Faithful Geyser." In retrospect this seems one of Yellowstone's least interesting features. An extensive boardwalk and seating constructed all around its base to accommodate the large number of onlookers give the area a man-made appearance.

Returning to the lodge I checked into my cabin, took time to dry out my tent from the rainy night before, and enjoyed a much needed hot shower. The balance of the day was spent relaxing and establishing my itinerary for the next few days.

I was up by dawn for a drive around the Old Faithful basin, which includes dozens of other geysers and geothermal features. Within this surreal landscape I took numerous short walks to specific sites. Over half of Yellowstone is a volcanic crater or caldron, formed by a cataclysmic eruption 600,000 years ago; active hot springs, fumaroles, and geysers are active reminders that all is not dormant. Walking about these bubbling infernos, one is actually on the floor of a volcanic remnant! Yellowstone's management should be commended for making these remarkable volcanic phenomena accessible to all. Boardwalks and walkways, all handicapped accessible, are located off the main roadway so it is not necessary to hike to them, although opportunities for that exist and make for an enhanced experience.

I hiked to several geysers (bear spray in hand), which were noteworthy for their diversity. In addition to seeing the geysers, etc., I drove on the main park road enjoying a plethora of wildlife, especially buffalo. The latter were all over the place. Without exaggeration I would say the worst traffic jam I have experienced west of the Mississippi River was in Yellowstone. This was not caused by cars, but a "buffalo jam" that occurs whenever a herd of buffalo (small or large) decides they want to stroll along the roadway at their own pace. I could only imagine what it must be like in the summer with hundreds of autos trying to move along Yellowstone's main route.

Fig. 31 - Buffalo share a principal road through Yellowstone National Park

I continued to the Canyon Rim Drive where there were several lookout points with views of the canyon and the falls of the Yellowstone River. I took brief walks on the rim trail to popular observation areas such as Inspiration Point, Grandview Point, and Artist Point, the latter offering the best overall view of the canyon. Unfortunately the weather was cold, dank and rainy; I really couldn't muster any enthusiasm for sloshing about the trails, so instead I headed to Yellowstone Lake. Along the snow covered shores of the still frozen lake I stopped for my typical camp lunch.

Eventually I arrived at Mammoth Hot Springs in the northern portion of the park, where I opted to check into the lodge rather than camp at the one open campground in that area because the weather was uncertain that evening. It turned out to be a good decision. While I was dining at the lodge around 9:00 p.m., a severe thunderstorm came rumbling through.

Earlier that evening I had taken a brief drive to the game-rich Lamar Valley to acquaint myself with the area. On my return, with a setting sun and dark thunder clouds forming on the horizon, I spotted several elk on the hillside. As I stopped to view them, the sun briefly broke through the cloud mist and a double rainbow was visible as a backdrop to the grazing elk, I scene which I successfully captured on film. I returned to *Mammoth Lodge* for a mediocre dinner and retired early because I wanted to be on the road by 5:30 the next morning to see the wildlife. In one sense such a drive wasn't necessary to see some large animals; outside my cabin door at dusk an adult buffalo foraged in the grass, oblivious to my stares.

The storm of the previous evening brought in a high pressure system and I was on the road by daybreak to the Lamar Valley under crystal clear blue skies with pleasant temperatures. As my drive continued east into the heart of the valley, I was awestruck by its beauty: snowcapped mountains in the background and with the seasonal snow melt, green hillsides and lush valleys below. With scattered herds of buffalo and elk the landscape took on the appearance of a mini Serengeti.

Soon I came upon a dozen or more cars parked on the roadside with scopes and telescopic cameras directed to the northern hillside. A fresh elk kill was being challenged by two grizzlies and four gray wolves; nobody knew which was responsible for taking down the elk. The scene was quite a distance away, and just who ended up with the choice cut of elk was still undetermined when I departed the scene a half hour later.

Fig. 32 - Wildlife observers viewing predator/prey interactions in Yellowstone's Lamar Valley

In Mammoth Hot Springs I went on a five-mile hike to an area of active beaver dams. The trail passed through a diverse landscape: Douglas fir stands, aspen groves, grassy meadows with budding wildflowers, and sagebrush covered plateaus with panoramic views. I spotted several mule deer and a pronghorn. It was an idyllic scene, made all the more so by the warmth of the sun shining through the deep blue sky. It was a walk in MY Garden of Eden. A bit teary-eyed, I reflected on my life: its past (with Loretta), the present (without her), and my future.

I reminisced over the many walks Loretta and I had taken together like I had in the redwoods earlier in the trip. I recalled our five-mile hike in a southern Rhode Island wildlife refuge in early spring of 1990 along with our daughter's cocker spaniel, Tracie. A wrong turn on the trail (my call) rerouted us for an estimated nine-mile trek back to our starting point. All survived, but Cher never left Tracie with us after that.

Then there was the time in 1985 in Thailand when I hired a small boat and its driver to take us to a remote, palm-studded island off the coast. I thought it would be an unforgettably romantic experience. Unforgettable, yes! Romantic, I don't think so! We arrived on shore expecting some type of concession offering food and drink; we had neither. A picture sign posted on the edge of the jungle showed a person with a rifle and a large "X" underneath. "No Trespassing!" With no shade nearby, the powdery, white sand and azure waters quickly lost their appeal and if our boat had not returned three hours later, Loretta and I might have become models for the movie *Castaway* !

But most of our walks were fun, relaxing, and provided pleasant moments together. I was experiencing comparable situations, but without Loretta.

At the same time, I remained thankful for the good fortune that shaped my life to date. Considering that Loretta and I were married as teenagers with all the attendant responsibilities of parenthood, while still needing to grow up ourselves and manage a household, we made out pretty well. I was fortunate to have had a successful career in the diamond industry, moving forward in twenty-five years from a lab technician to ultimately the President/CEO of Amplex Corp. Our technology for sizing diamond powders and the resulting products were recognized worldwide and attracted the attention of an acquisition-minded, multi-national company to whom we later sold our business. The transaction was financially rewarding to me and I continued to manage the business for our new owners while Loretta and I increased the frequency of our adventure travels. We had the financial freedom, and until 1992, the good health to do so. That it all changed with Loretta's illness cannot detract from those precious times.

On balance, I remain grateful for being where I am; so much of life is just being in the right place at the right time, enjoying the love of a good woman. I ponder my future with optimism, but temper it with the knowledge that my life will be quite different, less certain, and will offer many new and different opportunities and challenges.

I returned to Mammoth Hot Springs village for a brief lunch, then hiked to the nearby geyser basins, over and along the boardwalk which framed these geothermal wonders. The terraced, intricate mazes of formations were spectacular, confirmed by the continuous line of tourists sharing the trail; too crowded for me, so I returned to the Lamar Valley.

Weary from my earlier hikes, I found a quiet turnoff to take my customary half-hour power nap before commencing for a hike to Lost Lake. It wasn't especially challenging physically, but the opportunity to see black bear, known to frequent the area, raised my level of excitement. Armed with my bear bells, pepper spray, and a loud mouth, I headed out singing choruses of *It's a Wonderful World.* Whenever I came upon an area on the trail with a blind turn, I announced "COMING THROUGH" (a favorite expression of the park rangers,) very loudly so as not to surprise any bears. It seemed to work since I was following a set of fresh bear tracks without coming upon their makers. There was also a larger set of grizzly bear prints I'd seen at the start; thankfully they were now gone, as was the bear. As it was nearing sunset, I remained in my car after returning to the trail head and after fifteen minutes, a large black bear did appear on the trail about fifty yards from where I was observing. I watched for half an hour while he (or she) foraged along the moist grassy ravine below me. It was a pleasant, rewarding, and safe ending to a full and wonderfully enriching day.

The following morning, I was on the road at 5:30 heading once again into the Lamar Valley, where I stopped for a short, but very steep hike to Hell's Gate Suspension Bridge, which crosses the Yellowstone

River. In those wee hours of the morning, I did plenty of singing and talking along the desolate trail to avoid any surprise bear sightings.

Further up the road was a trailhead with several elk resting nearby and I noticed a hand-written sign warning of a grizzly sighting two days earlier. Would this be my chance to see one in the wild? Armed with my bear spray, I cautiously started down the path. After going about a quarter mile, I realized a stiff breeze was blowing…at me! Being downwind, my scent may not have been detectable and if I surprised a bear and sprayed it, two events would most likely occur: first, I would be on the receiving end of the spray. Secondly, if that didn't incapacitate me, the bear would!

Soon after I pulled off the road to watch first one, then two, and finally three, coyotes cross the road in front of me and continue across the meadows where they negotiated the shallows of the Lamar River toward a scattered herd of buffalo with several calves. Meanwhile, other cars had pulled over, with their binocular-clad occupants intently scanning the landscape. Concurrently, a pack of four gray wolves moved toward an elk herd in the distance. While a lone wolf chased the herd trying to separate one of the elk, three others waited on the downside in the wooded foothills just out of vision of the spotting scopes. We never knew if the wolves were successful.

As that event unfolded, the three coyotes earlier seen stalking the buffalo herd quickly and proficiently took down an unattended elk calf among the buffalo. Observers theorized its mother may have been the victim of the bears or wolves seen the previous day. It seemed to me like America's version of Africa's Serengeti!

With the drama over I continued to a trailhead leading to the Trout Pond set in the northeastern portion of Yellowstone. It was a bucolic setting with a crystal clear pond, surrounded by grassy meadows ringed with fir trees. Egg laying time for the fish was approaching and small schools of cutthroat trout could be seen in the shallows of the pond. This fresh water member of the salmon family is one of many trout sub-species and similar in appearance to the rainbow trout. It is a hard-fighting fish sought after by sport fisherman. After my hike, the sunny, warm afternoon beckoned me to indulge in an afternoon siesta. I laid there, knowing they were my final hours in Yellowstone. The past few days had filled my mind with treasured and lasting memories. My travels throughout the park viewing the wildlife in their natural habitat and hiking varied trails with the fear and excitement of possible bear encounters satisfied my innate sense of adventure. The diverse, natural landscape features of Yellowstone -- geothermal geysers and craters; the lush, green, wildlife-laden Lamar Valley; and deeply-eroded canyons and swiftly moving waters -- all instilled in me a reverence for its grandeur.

My nap on the bank of Trout Pond was interrupted by three large bull buffalo grazing on my sleeping grounds and oblivious to my presence. Given their unpredictability, I decided discretion was the better part of valor and quickly departed, but not without some excellent photos of these Yellowstone residents. As I returned to my car to exit the park, a female moose watched me drive away.

I continued east to Cody, WY, along the Chief Joseph highway, a particularly scenic route through the mountains and named for the chief of the Nez Perce Indians. After refusing to be sent to an Idaho reservation in 1877, he famously led eight hundred of his people toward freedom at the Canadian border with two thousand U.S. soldiers in pursuit. His brave and skillful attempts to evade the pursuing army impressed even his adversaries, but after a brutal five-day battle in freezing weather and with no food and blankets, Chief Joseph formally surrendered to General Miles on October 5, 1877. Although it was his understanding that he and his people would be allowed to return home, that, not surprisingly, did not come to pass. They were shuffled about several reservations where many died from endemic diseases. Chief Joseph, still in exile from his homeland, passed away in 1904 "of a broken heart," according to his doctor.

Upon arriving in Cody, I checked into the *Irma Hotel*, Cody's most famous landmark. Built by Buffalo Bill Cody and named for his daughter, the original building and much of its former contents remain today.

The next day I toured several interesting western theme places, the most notable and extensive being the Buffalo Bill Historical Center, a complex of five different museums. Together they tell the story of the west, Bill Cody, the Plains Indians, and all that was part of this region's historical lore. I made a brief but memorable late afternoon visit to "Trail Town," an engaging collection of old buildings moved to the western edge of Cody from northwest Wyoming and southern Montana. Some of these structures have historical significance (such as one used by Butch Cassidy and The Sundance Kid as a hideaway). The memorial cemetery holds the remains of several Wild West figures, including those of the famous mountain man, Jeremiah Johnson, portrayed by Robert Redford in a movie. He also served as a pallbearer when Johnson's remains were moved to Trail Town.

That evening at the hotel bar I had an interesting discussion about bear pepper spray with a few of the patrons, all Cody residents. I recounted my experiences at Yellowstone where I hiked several trails, confident my bear spray would provide any needed defense against grizzlies. After all, wasn't that why it was sold in the park? I was chided about my naiveté, and a consensus quickly emerged that was best conveyed by the bartender: "If you're in grizzly territory with pepper spray in one hand, you better have a rifle in the other hand! And a large caliber one at that!" Though I questioned the legitimacy of his statement, I was glad I hadn't heard it *before* my Yellowstone adventures.

The next morning I began my northerly route toward Montana through and over the Bighorn Mountain Range. My first stop was at Shell Falls, a 120- ft. waterfall pouring out 3,600 gallons of water every second, cascading into the geologically impressive Shell Canyon. It was an imposing scene, torrents of water hurdling into the vast canyon below.

I reached my Montana destination for that day, the Little Bighorn National Monument, which was scene of General George Custer's overwhelming defeat by a band of Sioux Indians led by Chief Crazy Horse in 1876. The road that wound through the battlefield had site markers laid out with historical accuracy, made possible after prairie fires in the mid 1980s ravaged the area and destroyed all vegetation. Extensive archaeological recovery operations located many artifacts, including animal and human skeletal remains, which have been forensically analyzed and identified to place them, along with other items, in their exact location at the time of the battle. An interpretative center and museum is on the premises as well. A visitor may come away with an unsettling understanding of the events leading to the battle as well as the post battle period that sadly led to closing the final chapter on the Plains Indians. I was moved by the overall presentation and noted that in the recreation of this event, General Custer loses (and deservedly so) his hero status. Current interpretation of this tragic event provides a more balanced picture and is more sensitive to Native Americans than had previously been the case.

Fig. 33 - Battle site at Little Big Horn on Crow Indian Reservation, Crow Agency, MT

Little Bighorn is located on 700,000 acres of the Crow Indian Reservation. I visited Crow Agency, the town center of the reservation and home to Little Bighorn College. I introduced myself and inquired if I might speak with someone regarding the life and culture of Crow as they are today. I was introduced to Lani Realbird, a business teacher at the college who suggested I speak with some of the tribal elders. Since it was late afternoon, I found lodging in nearby Harden and returned the following morning to speak with Corky Oldhorn and Darrin Old Coyote as well as Kathleen, a non-native math teacher at the two year college. Apart from the usual issues that face many communities (economics, jobs, crime, and health), a major concern of the residents is a cultural one, viz, fewer of the younger generation are able to speak their native Crow (Apsaalooke) language. Crow is the most widely spoken native language in Montana, and the older people believe strongly that *"language is the voice of our culture."* Apparently, a principal reason for the decline of native language skills is the young people's belief that speaking Crow makes it more difficult to blend with the world outside the reservation. Their language consists of many words difficult to pronounce, and mispronunciation of a syllable can alter the meaning of an entire thought. Tribal adults can be especially critical of such errors and do not lightly dismiss them, placing further pressure on their children.

I bid a grateful farewell to those who had extended me their time and drove back to Harden where I spent a second night. The next morning I couldn't resist a visit to a western outfitter's clothing store in the modest downtown area where I ended up spending a couple of hours conversing with Sal, the engaging female proprietor and two of her regular men folk who socialize there daily. By the time I left the store I had purchased an Alaskan outfitter's hat and with Sal's assistance booked a local guide for a trip down the nearby Big Horn River to test my fly fishing skills in its trout-laden waters the next day.

At the Bighorn Canyon National Recreational area overlooking the scenic Bighorn River, I set up camp for the evening. In this instance, as well as all my overnight camping, "setting up" is merely pitching a one person fly tent (five minutes, maximum) and adding the air mattress (now useless), sleeping bag, blanket, pillow, and flashlights inside (two more minutes). After a moderate hike to and from the reservoir end of the canyon, I retired for the evening and had a surprisingly good night's sleep. I was only awakened by strong winds that continued into the day and made for some challenging fly fishing.

By 9 o'clock I was drifting down the Bighorn River with my guide and his sixteen-ft. flat bottom boat, casting left or right at his direction in search of those elusive trout. I soon discovered this style of fly fishing takes a skill and technique that I sorely lacked. Continuous winds of 20-30 knots didn't help, but since other fishermen were faring better than me, it is fair to assume my casting shortcomings could not be blamed on the wind.

In order to land the rainbow or brown trout, tiny nymph flies have to be presented in just the right way, the line "mended" as needed, and the rod positioned correctly to set the hook when struck; it wasn't easy. For every one fish I landed, I failed to set the hook on maybe a dozen others. It was frustrating, as was having to continually remove bits of green algae from the fly's hook. But, when nearing the end of our run, on a delicate cast I had a hard hit that I responded to correctly for a change (an abrupt, timely lift of the rod's tip); and I finally had a big one on the other end. I kept the tip pointed up while letting my catch run at will. Ten minutes later my guide waded out in the river with net in hand to corral a beautiful twenty-four inch rainbow trout (and I've the picture to prove it)!

Coincidentally, this is the same guide operation used by President George Bush and his Vice President Richard Chaney on their trout fishing trips to this region.

I had planned to be in Bozeman, MT, that evening, two hundred miles west, so I called it quits and was on the road by 6 o'clock. With a posted speed limit of 75 mph (most vehicles were doing 85), I took the Interstate to Bozeman and arrived by 8:30. With Memorial Day weekend ahead and several events going on in Bozeman during that timeframe, available lodging was tight. I finally found accommodations and settled in for the evening. My departure from Bozeman the next morning followed a visit to the Museum of the Rockies located on the campus of Montana State University. It is an outstanding museum, which in addition to showcasing Montana's history, geology and cultural diversity, houses many exhibits relating to the Lewis and Clark Expedition (there are more Lewis and Clark sites in Montana than in any other state). There was also a comprehensive astronomy and cosmology display in conjunction in the planetarium. A paleontology exhibit highlighted the many fossil remains found and extracted from Montana's lands. This modern, well organized museum is under the auspices of the University and is an affiliate of the Smithsonian Institution.

On the road east of Billings and above the bottom lands of the Yellowstone River was Pompey's Pillar, a huge sandstone outcropping bearing the only remaining physical evidence of Lewis and Clark's expedition route. On the face of this one-hundred-fifty-ft. mass of rock, William Clark carved his name and date (WM. Clark July 23, 1806) on his return trip. The pillar was named for Sacagawea's son, who Clark nicknamed "Pomp." I climbed to its summit; the view remains much as it was when Clark stood there looking out toward the Bighorn Mountains, the plains, and the meandering course of the Yellowstone River.

Fig. 34 - Pompey's Pillar with inscription denoting passage of William Clark on eastward return, near Billings, MT

Continuing east I stopped at Miles City, considered to be one of the last genuine cowboy towns in the west. The Range Rider museum on the outskirts of town has a collection of western memorabilia of all kinds, including many late 19th-century photographs of Native Americans and other historically interesting people of Miles City and the surrounding areas. Among the photos was the last picture taken of Will Rogers prior to his ill-fated Alaskan air flight. I stopped for a beer at a local saloon on the modest main street and was surprised to see so few people around on a late Friday afternoon. No "Happy Hours" there!

Since I had an hour's drive ahead of me to my evening destination of Makoshika State Park in the badlands region of eastern Montana, I didn't linger. I arrived there at dusk to set up my tent as the only camper in the park. Makoshika defined all the features of an eroded, badlands landscape, including pinnacles and all shapes of buttes and boulders. At the lower levels fossil beds contained dinosaur bones from tyrannosaurs, triceratops, and other large dinosaurs who once roamed that region.

I awoke to a chilly start to the Memorial Day weekend and immediately drove to the Cap Rock Nature Trail for a two-mile hike through a sculptured rock garden of eroded features of varying eccentric forms with names like rain pillars, baked potatoes, toad stools, popcorn, and more. Another trail, Kinney Coulee, descended over 300 feet to the base of the badlands where a fully intact triceratops skull was found just below the surface in 1990. I saw nothing of the kind on my descent to the floor of the canyon, but the weirdly- shaped sandstone buttes all around, coupled with the total solitude of the early morning, suggested an extraterrestrial landscape.

I returned to the Visitor Center to see the exhibits and peruse a comprehensive mural depicting the geology and paleontology of the region. Within the center was the display of the complete Triceratops skull noted earlier, as well as other exhibits describing current fossil digs under the auspices of the Museum of the Rockies.

It was a long, nondescript ride through the rolling, endless prairie land of northern North Dakota before I reached the Missouri River and followed it along the Lewis and Clark Trail past Sacagawea Lake to the Knife River Indian Villages. There were remains of three Hidatsa communities where the tribes lived in large dome-like structures known as earthen lodges. This was the village where Sacagawea lived before she joined the Lewis and Clark Expedition. Only the site remains from the original village and consists of circular depressions on the ground that would have been a lodge location. There is a splendid, meticulously furnished, ful-scale reproduction of an earthen lodge that gives the visitor a fascinating insight into the life of the village. I took a meandering walk around the area to absorb some of the history of this site.

There were other Lewis and Clark sites in the area near Washburn, ND. I arrived there after visiting hours and checked into a roadside motel, planning to visit the sites the following day. The evening concluded with dinner at a local bar and grill with cash prize bingo being played in the well-worn, bustling dining room of *Captain's Cabin*. A juicy, tasty, inexpensive prime rib was extraordinary and much enjoyed despite the smoke-heavy atmosphere.

The next morning I visited the Lewis and Clark Interpretative Center at the outskirts of town. Nearby was Fort Mandan a reconstructed fort several miles up the river from where its original had been located. Because of the flow change in the Missouri River over the past couple of hundred years, the original site is no longer a land area, hence the need to reconstruct Mandan on an alternate site. This fort was significant to Lewis and Clark, because they wintered here for 146 days before setting out on their journey. Fort Mandan was where many of the initial preparations were made, and relationships were established with the neighboring Mandan and Hidatsa Indians who provided the group with much information regarding the lands and tribes to the west. It was also here that Lewis hired the trader Charbonneau as a guide, accompanied by his Shoshone Indian squaw wife Sacagawea, who gave birth to their son while wintering with the Corps of Discovery at Fort Mandan. It was the longest occupied site on the expedition, and it was here that Sacagawea, Charbonneau, and their son Jean Baptiste bid farewell to the group after the expedition was concluded.

The interpretive center had a full-sized piroit, or dugout canoe, constructed to the exact dimensions and details of those used by the Corps of Discovery. Accompanying the model was a detailed, pictorial "how to build" display showing it being made and moved into place when this center was constructed a few years ago. Having already been to several Lewis & Clark Centers, I was impressed how they all, despite essentially covering the same topics, managed to differentiate themselves.

My next stop was the capital city of North Dakota, Bismarck, whose nineteen-story rectangular capitol building seemed devoid of any character. Within the capitol complex was the North Dakota Heritage Center, a showcase for the state's historical society. The museum depicted the history of North Dakota chronologically from its geologic beginnings to the present, with considerable emphasis on the settling of North Dakota during the western movement of the 1800s. A collection of early photographs and personal chronicles provided accounts of the early settlers and told a compelling story of the challenges facing these people in their harsh environment. All of the seasons presented challenges. Winters had temperatures to minus 40° F; spring brought severe hail storms; insect and mosquito infestations of unimaginable severity occurred during the summer months. One quoted account from 1880 speaks of mosquitoes so thick on the wagon mules that one could not see the color of the mules. The same journal describes settlers being bitten through several layers of clothing, even through the eyelets in their shoes!

The Heritage Center also had a gallery where the artistry of George Chapman was on display. Chapman had ventured west in the late 1820s to capture the native people and their customs on canvas. After his death in 1872, the Smithsonian requested and received many of his works for its permanent collection. The Heritage Society presentation was well worth the visit and reinforced my enthusiasm for experiencing the essence of a community by seeking out its local museums. The richness and content of the exhibits inevitably impress.

Back on the road I drove south to Theodore Roosevelt National Park in the Badlands of North Dakota. It was there that Theodore Roosevelt visited our country's wild west for his first time while in his early twenties. He built a cabin and a ranch, then he became a cattle rancher and shot his first buffalo there. Roosevelt's fondness for this region is well documented in his prolific writings. En route to the Black Hills I listened to David McCullough's audio book, *Morning on Horseback*, which chronicled T.R.'s earlier times and experiences and provided me background information about the area and Roosevelt's influence on it.

I arrived late in the day and set up my tent in one of the two campgrounds and took a brief walk around Madera, the gateway town to the park. In the style of a western town, Madera had its complement of restaurants and shops neatly arranged along its few streets, and I took supper at a pizza-style deli before I returned to camp and retired for the night.

I was off at daybreak and drove within the park to various trail heads where the hikes were essentially nature walks with marked posts indicating the geology and flora of the area. It was not that much of a physical workout, but alone and in the vastness of the panorama unfolding before me it was a wonderfully tranquil experience. This was classic badlands territory with brick-red rocks providing the brightest colors to the landscape.

During my leisurely drive along the park's scenic roadway, I saw my first "Prairie Dog Town." The name describes open, nearly grassless land with mounded entrances to the tunneled homes of colonies of prairie dogs that were all over the place, scurrying underground at the least provocation. I sat for several entertaining minutes watching and photographing their antics.

At the Visitor Center there was an impressive collection of personal artifacts and photos of Roosevelt from his many visits to the badlands. Of the two ranch homes he had here, the smaller Maltese Cross Cabin, was moved adjacent to the center and is open to the public. It holds several of the original furnishings and household items used by T.R. during his stay. All that remains of his other home, Elkhorn Ranch, is an undeveloped site several miles north.

The ride to Deadwood, two hundred miles south, passed through rolling green prairies occupied mostly by beef cattle with the occasional sheep herds and scattered horse farms. Deadwood is the quintessential tourist city living off its Wild West reputation. With several re-created buildings and activities intended to revitalize its colorful past, it nonetheless caters to 21st-century America's appetite for gaming. There are some authentic artifacts in various museums, and the nearby Mount Morah Cemetery holds the remains of some famous and notorious western characters. But Deadwood is about gaming. Limited stakes gambling returned to Deadwood in 1989 and most public establishments along the single main street have gaming tables and slot machines.

Being the Memorial Day weekend the town was teeming with tourists and after an overnight at a downtown hotel/casino, I moved on early the next morning to Mount Rushmore after a brief stop at the Mount Morah Cemetery. The most prominent of the grave sites contained the remains of Wild Bill Hickok and Calamity Jane, the latter buried alongside Wild Bill at her request.

It was a day steeped in Americana. My first stop (as the gates were opening) was Mount Rushmore, our country's memorial to four of its greatest leaders. Carving the mountain was originally the idea of Doane Robinson, a South Dakota historian and tourist promoter who was looking for a means of attracting more visitors to the state. He wanted to see regionally significant persons represented in the sculpturing such as Lewis and Clark, George Custer, Wild Bill Hickok, and others. He contacted Idaho-born sculptor Gutzon Borglum, who, instead, insisted the figures must be those of national notoriety. Gutzon's selections were intended to recognize each president's particular significance: George Washington was our first president and father of our country (FOUNDING); Thomas Jefferson doubled its size with the purchase of the Louisiana Territory (EXPANSION); Abraham Lincoln is credited with holding the nation together during the Civil War (PRESERVATION); and Theodore Roosevelt was responsible for the construction of the Panama Canal (DEVELOPEMENT).

Two bits of trivia regarding the sculpturing of the Presidents' faces stay with me. Firstly, ninety percent of the work was accomplished with dynamite; secondly, for most of the project those assigned work on the presidents' profiles had to ascend 760 steep steps to get to their work area (pay time did not begin until they began work). Each day it was up that many, then down, all on the workers' time!

Of the 395 workers who had at one time or another been on the payroll, one who was employed on the project from 1939-1940 was on hand to sell and sign a modest booklet he and his wife put together a few years ago. The booklet answered most of the commonly asked questions about Mount Rushmore, including:

1) How long did it take? (Overall, fourteen years)

2) When was it dedicated? (July 4, 1930)

3) How did it get its name? (Charles Rushmore, an attorney with no ties to the project)

4) What is the height of Mt. Rushmore? (5,725 feet)

5) How much did it cost? ($990,000 – in 1930 dollars)

Don "Nick" Clifford was an engaging, personable eighty-four years young when I met him, and I peppered him with many questions about the project.

I asked Nick whether masks were used by the men to protect against the dust inevitably generated by the drilling; silicosis must have been a danger. He said they were available but most chose not to use them because they clogged up too fast! (Um…..isn't that a good reason to wear them?) When that question was posed to him, he responded with a shrug and said, "I'm still here." And, I might add, with a charming, personable, and very attractive wife not all that much his junior. After finishing our conversation I thanked him for his contribution to the monument and departed Mount Rushmore for the Crazy Horse Memorial, fifteen miles away.

Conceived in the late 1930s by Lokota Indian Chief Henry Standing Bear in the late 1930s, this Herculean monument was begun a decade later by sculptor Korczak Ziolkowski (a Boston transplant from Poland). When completed, the memorial will depict Crazy Horse on his horse, left arm extended, responding to a white man's taunts just before his death in 1877. Its scale is mind-boggling: it will dwarf the Great Pyramid of

Giza and the Statue of Liberty. All four of Rushmore's presidents would fit inside Crazy Horse's head!

Fig. 35 – In-progress carvings of the Crazy Horse Memorial in the Black Hills of SD

Ziolkowski earlier refused money from the U.S. Government for his work, as have the present Indian nations, mistrustful of any such intervention by the Government that took this very land from them over a century ago. Instead the project is funded with private donations and contributions and progress is slow; consequently, only the face of Crazy Horse has been sculpted to date. The sculpture's son Casimir, 52, now oversees the effort.

There is a large visitor/museum/cultural center complex on site, and future plans call for a university and medical center as well. When I inquired of an Indian guide as to an expected completion date, there was none! My sense was that the Indians see this monument as a "work in progress," and with one million visitors annually (versus Mt.

Rushmore's three million), they see its gradual expansion as testimony to the commitment and perseverance of their people.

By afternoon though the day began rainy and cool, the sun was shining brightly with only a few fluffy cumulous clouds drifting by. Next on my agenda was Custer State Park in the heart of the Black Hills, a wild and beautiful region, thick with dark green forests of Ponderosa Pine whose color gives the hills their name. It is a geologic wonder of cracked limestone caves, conifer forests, huge granite monoliths, and boulders reaching skyward.

Despite warnings of imminent thunderstorms, I pitched my tent in the park's campground and left for a couple of short but strenuous hikes to the summits of adjacent mountains. One of the trails, Little Devils Tower, was only a mile to the top, but the very steep trail was a challenge. Once I'd reached the rocky summit, the view was worth the effort. As far as the eye could see were the undisturbed Black Hills: craggy mountains and cathedral-like spires of granite amid forests of Ponderosa Pines, whose dark, almost black appearance gives the name to this eight-thousand-square-mile stretch of land from eastern Wyoming to western South Dakota. It was an ideal spot to sit back, relax, appreciate the view, and ultimately dose off. (You get the feeling by now that I've a penchant for naps).

Returning to my campsite I took a hot shower and laundered my clothes at a nearby lakeside cottage resort; it was now after Memorial Day and the various services in the recreational areas were open for the season. I enjoyed a walleye fish dinner at the *Lakeside Lodge* on Sylvan Lake just outside Custer State Park and after that I was ready to retire for the night.

My hikes of the previous day were the last of my mountain adventures. I subsequently moved into the northern plains and prairies of Nebraska and Iowa. I had been in, around, and up and down the mountains and canyons of the southwest, the west, and the northwest parts of our country ever since I left San Antonio in mid-February. I was ready for a change, at least from a topological perspective, so I left Custer State Park at daybreak for the short drive to Wind Cave National Park. My route included the Wildlife Loop of Custer State Park, so named because of the large buffalo herds grazing on its parklands, which shared the prairie with mule deer, pronghorn antelope, donkeys, and prairie dogs, among others. The Loop eventually reached and became part of Wind Cave National Park. The Visitors Center was situated at the entrance to these unique caverns which encompass over 100 miles of known passages. These caves differ from most others because there is relatively little moisture within their limestone sanctuaries, so there are not the typical stalagmite/stalactite formations. There are unique, artistic calcite growths known by names such as boxworks, popcorn, and needles. The ninety- minute, ranger-guided tour through the caverns provided a thorough explanation of their geology, history, and the ongoing efforts of exploration and conservation. The name "Wind Cave" describes the air movement created because the cavern's atmospheric pressure seeks to balance with the above ground air pressure (the caves have many natural openings). Wind Cave National Park is relatively small, but with its large buffalo population and fascinating subterranean passageways, it warrants more attention from tourists.

I called my mother later that day to tell her of my general whereabouts. Incredulously, her first words were: "Did you go to Wind Cave?" Unbelievable! Here is an eighty-eight-year-old, great-grandmother living in an assisted-living center and using its library seeking the latest issues of *National Park* magazine to keep track of my whereabouts. When I told her, she wanted to know more about the boxworks formations!

Mom grew up in the depression era and the economic circumstances of her family dictated that work take precedence over school. Her formal education ended after the ninth grade. She once told me what a sad time that was for her because she loved school and the opportunity to learn about anything and everything. In all the years that I can recall, mom was a prolific reader, observer, and conversationalist who educated herself on a myriad of subjects. Her ongoing pursuit to learn new things and keep her mind active and keen has been an inspiration to me and, thankfully, part of my genetic makeup.

I preceded to Hot Springs, SD, for lunch and a tour of Mammoth Site, an excavated area on the outskirts of town holding the remains of fifty prehistoric Columbian and Woolly mammoths. The fossilized skeletons were exposed but left intact within the sedimentary material just as they were found. There are extensive fossil deposits throughout this entire region.

South from Hot Springs was Wounded Knee, SD, site of a tragic massacre of Indians by the U.S. Calvary in 1889 that outraged the American public. Wounded Knee is a hamlet with several ramshackle homes, a general store, and a post office, which could be a shantytown leftover, scattered alongside unimproved dirt roads. A small cemetery on a knoll in the center of Wounded Knee contained the remains of Indians who were killed in that battle as well as recent tribal burials of former residents. Walking among the gravesites, I was immediately joined by several youths, who came out of nowhere. They were soliciting money for their baseball team, though I saw no evidence of baseball anywhere. I happily contributed to their coffers, hoping the money would find good use. The cemetery grounds showed no signs of upkeep and the appearance was consistent with the depressed landscape in that area. I saw no memorial commemorating the tragedy of Wounded Knee.

Fig. 36 - Cemetery of old and new gravesites at Wounded Knee on Pine Ridge Indian Reservation, SD

I joined with Route 20 for the eastward drive along Nebraska's northern countryside and passed what seemed like an endless stretch of cattle ranches. I stopped in the small town of Valentine, "The Heart of the Sand Hills," and center of the region's extensive cattle ranching industry. The Sand Hills are a unique feature of the Nebraska ecosystem and consist of extensive sand dunes formed of wind blown sand from an ancient sea and now covered with a grassy overgrowth that stabilizes them from the howling plains' wind. Nearby is said to be the world's largest aquifer, Ogallala, a vast, shallow water table lying beneath 174,000 square miles in portions of eight states: Texas, New Mexico, Oklahoma, Kansas, Colorado, Wyoming, South Dakota, and Nebraska. The marshes and low meadows overlying it provide home to a wide variety of birds and mammals.

I checked into a motel in Valentine, a town also known for the number of Valentine Day cards postmarked there. The following morning provided an opportunity for an early walk along "Cowboy Trail," a pathway running along the outskirts of Valentine and past a large area of cattle pens where a cattle auction was to take place that morning. I was told a superb breakfast was available at the auction site, so I checked out of my motel and went to that cafeteria, a sparse room with an institutional type kitchen and several cowboys at the tables. Across the hallway was the auction pit where the bidding would be starting shortly. I ordered a full breakfast of sausage, eggs, potatoes, and the usual fixings. I can state, unequivocally, it was the best breakfast of its kind I'd ever had. If ever an ordinary breakfast could taste extraordinary, this one surely did!

Outside at the cattle pens I watched the ranchers unload their unwanted bulls and cows and then leave, resigned to accept whatever winning bids came forth. I saw a handsome-looking bull being off-loaded from one of the trailers and asked its owner why he was going to auction. His reply was that he bought it for breeding purposes and the bull wouldn't breed! Despite the temptations of several cows, the bull showed no interest. I asked if there was a cattle version of Viagra on the market. He laughed and then commented that expenses of any type were always a consideration and other accommodating bulls were available. He also glibly questioned that bull's sexual orientation.

In the auction pit were four buyers acting on behalf of meat packing firms. The animals, one or two at a time, were directed into the pit where an auctioneer mumbled what were to me unintelligible callings. It was fascinating to watch these proceedings and I'm sure I looked like a potential buyer with my cowboy hat, vest, and boots; I was careful not to make any gestures for fear I'd own one of the four-legged beasts.

Fig. 37 - Cattle pit for livestock auctions, Valentine, NE

Departing Valentine, I continued eastward through several hamlets, eventually detouring to the Ashfall Fossil Beds, a state park with an unusual and very extensive collection of fossilized North American mammals, including rhinos, three toed horses, and camels. What makes the site different is that the animals were fossilized as a result of a rapid descent of ash from a volcano in what is now Idaho, a volume hundreds of times greater than that that spewed from Mount St. Helens in 1980. Traveling over great distances, the ash quickly compacted over the grazing animals to depths of several feet. For ten million years the amazingly well-preserved skeletons of these prehistoric mammals lay undisturbed under a blanket of volcanic particles. Because the surrounding material is easily removed, the carcass remains are largely intact upon excavation and provide a wealth of information to paleontologists. This feature of the site attracts prominent scientists from around the world.

Walking around the area surrounding the Visitor Center, I could see several partially exposed fossils in the process of being uncovered by visiting scientists and their student assistants. It was very much a work in progress.

I left Ashfall, traveling for Stone State Park, outside Sioux City, IA. It is situated within the geologically distinctive Loess Hills, an area where glacial activities of the past deposited fertile soils to depths of 100 feet and more, a land form duplicated in only one other place in the world (along the Yellow River in China). Finding the park's location even with my GPS and On Star assistance was a challenge, but ultimately I arrived, set up camp in late afternoon, and idled away the remaining hours of daylight. Sardines and crackers were my dinner choice, which was sufficient after my sumptuous breakfast at the Valentine auction.

A postscript to my drive through Nebraska: I expected a lengthy and boring period of travel through the cornfields, cattle ranches, and prairies, but the several stops I made in the small towns along Route 20 proved to be enriching experiences; the places were interesting and the people friendly and outgoing. I really enjoyed meeting and talking with them. I especially recall my stop at a 1950s style soda shop in O'Neil to satisfy my urge for a strawberry milkshake. While I was conversing with the counter clerk, an affable, talkative elderly lady came in. She was a well known customer and was promptly asked about the previous night's police sirens and commotion at the nearby retirement home where she resides.

According to her recount of the incident two of the men living there became physical with each other when one of them was overly affectionate to the other's "lady friend." For whatever reason the staff could not quell the disturbance and police had to be called. It reminded me of a similar incident at my mother's assisted care facility the past year. In that case two female residents had designs on one of the men and were not bashful in displaying their jealous rages. Human sexual attitudes and desires seem less bounded by age than one might think.

Listening to mom's portrayal of those exploits gave me hope that some exciting times await me in old age.

Anyhow, back in Iowa, during the night at my Stone Park camp there were strong thunderstorms and I surprised myself with the ease that I was able to sleep through most of it. At daybreak I hiked along a nature trail, not a particularly interesting one in comparison with earlier hikes in more geographically diverse regions.

After breaking camp I visited the park's nature center, containing exhibits covering the geology, history, flora, and fauna of the region. Prominently noted on the museum's bulletin board was what might best be described as "media-hyped" coverage of mountain lion sightings in the surrounding urban area in late 2004. There was an incident where a lioness had to be killed while up a tree in a residential neighborhood. Apparently, using a tranquilizer gun was not safe because no one could predict how the cat would react before succumbing to the drug. Being in a populated environment she could pose a danger to those nearby, so the authorities had little choice.

Before leaving Sioux City, I sought out the highly regarded public museum housed in a turn-of-the-century city mansion. The exhibits emphasized Sioux City's history, especially during the late 19ᵗʰ century when it was one of our country's leading commercial centers, thanks to its stockyards and meat packing industry. The lore of Sioux City professional baseball for over a century was recounted with pictorial and written accounts of its teams in great detail. I'm sure my son would have been enthralled with this account of Sioux City baseball, given his love of the game and appreciation of its history.

A long uneventful ride east took me to Dyersville, IA, site of the Iowa cornfield-turned-baseball diamond in the classic baseball movie, *Field of Dreams.* Unknown to me until I tried to get a motel for the night, Dyersville is also known as the "Farm Toy Capital of the World," and that weekend was the semi-annual farm toy show. Several hundred exhibitors displayed their collectible miniatures in numerous buildings and vendor carts scattered all about this small town. A tractor parade was scheduled for the next evening, but with the threat of thunderstorms imminent I decided I would pass up the event. I bought a miniature replica of the tractor used by Kevin Costner's movie character. It was for John, a good baseball buddy, fellow golfer, and farm implement aficionado, who sat beside me at an historic Red Sox game while we belted out the chords of Neil Diamond's *Sweet Caroline* in the bottom of the 8th at Fenway! We've been buddies ever since.

In a steady rain the following morning I drove several miles past cornfields to the "Field of Dreams." I thought it unusual that two separately-owned properties comprised the baseball field and farmhouse. The dividing lines are such that one souvenir store is in front of the farm house, while on the third base side of the diamond there is another souvenir shop run by the owners of that portion of the property. There is no admission charge to use the playing field, and visitors are encouraged to come with bat, ball, and glove.

From Dyersville I went to Dubuque and took a ride to the city summit via what is referred to as an inclined elevator, which is, in reality, an antiquated outdoor tram on rails. At the top the elevation afforded a good overview of the city looking west over the mighty Mississippi. Dubuque has an excellent four-year-old River Museum and Aquarium, which provided an in-depth treatise on all aspects of the river. It was an informative half-day, self-guided tour covering this country's most dominant water feature and the famous personalities associated with it, among them Mark Twain and Louis Armstrong.

Entering Illinois, I encountered an unexpected gem, Galena, once a lead mining town and home to former U.S. President, Ulysses S. Grant. Though an obvious tourist draw, Galena has kept its architectural past well preserved, and the various stores, restaurants, gift shops, and galleries present themselves in an understated, authentic manner. Along the well- preserved Main Street was the historic *DeSoto Hotel*, a residence to presidents and persons of influence since the 1850s. I took the last available room at the *DeSoto* for that evening and walked from the hotel to the former home of U.S. Grant and his family. The Grants resided there for two years after the end of the Civil War, and the modestly proportioned mansion displayed several authentic pieces belonging to the Grant family.

Another nearby mansion, the largest house in Galena, was stuffed with antiques purchased by the current owners, who have lived there for thirty-five years. Some of the items were noteworthy, including a chair from the Vatican and several items purchased from MGM studios. Among the latter were green draperies from the movie set of *Gone with the Wind,* which were made into a dress in the movie by heroine Scarlet O'Hara. Despite the artifacts, the twenty-two room, 13,000-sq.-ft. mansion was so cluttered that its overall appearance was that of a high-priced flea market. I later learned that the owner/residents were antique dealers; I suspect this was merely a means of displaying their wares.

Later that evening I enjoyed one of the top ten meals of my travels, a Kansas strip steak at the *Backstreet Steak and Chop House.* My beef consumption in the Midwest will probably leave me with a case of gout and high cholesterol! In reality most of my meals were beefless and fish, salads, and fruit were the norm. My evening ended at an outdoor music festival in the center of town that highlighted Galena's inaugural "Lead Foot Motorcycle Rally Weekend." Get me my "Hog!"

After attending church services at a local Catholic church, I started towards Springfield, IL, along the Great River Road, which paralleled the Mississippi River. It was not an especially interesting road, but it kept me off the interstates that I strove to avoid. I arrived in Springfield by midday with my first stop being President Abraham Lincoln's tomb and a reverential tour of his final resting place. Located on the outskirts of the city and set in an expansive cemetery of stately trees and beautifully landscaped grounds, it is an ideal spot for the final resting place of one of our country's icons.

From there I checked into the downtown *Hilton Hotel*, a short walking distance to Lincoln's home, the State Capitol, and the new Lincoln Museum and Library. That afternoon I visited Lincoln's home, where he lived with his wife Mary Todd and their children for seventeen years, leaving only after his election as the sixteenth President.

I was disappointed with the presentation of the house and its furnishings during the tour. Given the importance and relevance of the subject, I thought it was one of the more lackluster tours I participated in during my entire trip. This may have been due to a National Park guide with limited knowledge of the site and a level of enthusiasm to match.

I continued with a walk about the center of Springfield to the State Capitol buildings, the new as well as the older, original structure. Later that evening, as I was contemplating my next destination, I considered moving northward, foregoing St. Louis, as I had seen plenty of Lewis and Clark interpretive centers on my journey and wasn't looking forward to driving in a big city.

However, I then noted on the sport page of the local newspaper that the Boston Red Sox would be in St. Louis for a three-game series, their first meeting since last year's World Series when the Bosox ended their eighty-six-year drought with a straight, four-game series win. It was a two-hour ride from Springfield to St. Louis so I decided I would go to the ball park and take my chances finding a ticket for the game that evening. First thing the next morning, while still in Springfield, I called ahead to reserve a room at a downtown St. Louis hotel within walking distance to both Busch Stadium and the famous Arch, which also houses the Western Museum featuring Lewis and Clark's Expedition.

I then went to the Lincoln Museum for its 9:00 a.m. opening, hoping to get started before the hoards of other tourists arrived. I only partially succeeded on that account; by 10:00 a.m. there was a sizable crowd of children and adults throughout the museum. Nonetheless, this was an extraordinary and very emotionally moving experience. In the museum proper, several rooms were constructed and furnished as they would have been during Lincoln's presidency. These included rooms from his early home, law office, the store he worked as a clerk, and several of those from the White House.

In each were life-size, wax figures depicting characters such as Lincoln and others who may have occupied those rooms. A favorite among visitors was the War Room of the White House showing Lincoln with several of his cabinet members in heated discussion. The theatrical presentations, short and well-scripted, and technologically very much 21st century did much to capture the essence of our sixteenth President.

Considerable space was allocated to the tragic story of our Civil War with emphasis on the Emancipation Proclamation, Gettysburg, and other notable confrontations during those years of 1861-1865, which were known to "try men's souls." There was a temporary exhibit provided by private collectors that rendered a timeline of events and characters surrounding the assassination of the President. Several original items from that tragic act were shown, including the bed in which Lincoln took his final breath.

In superlative fashion the museum tells the story of the U.S.A. at its most vulnerable time and the courage of one of our country's greatest leaders, a man who would not compromise his staunchly held convictions under the most unimaginably difficult and trying of circumstances. Certainly there was food for thought here as I continued to consider the questions I had posed for myself at the beginning of these travels. An account of Lincoln and his wartime cabinet, *Team of Rivals,* by Doris Kearns Goodwin, was published as my trip concluded. It dissects, analyzes, and recounts the extraordinary relationships Lincoln developed with key cabinet members and offers lasting lessons in leadership and personal relations under the most challenging of circumstances.

After lunch in the museum café I drove to St. Louis, where I checked into a downtown inn, and headed out to the ball park to locate a ticket for the game that night. Despite hearing on the local radio stations that there were absolutely no tickets available for the series' opening game, success came within the hour. I was able to get a field box ticket, not cheap by any standards, but worth it to a long-suffering Red Sox fan finally rewarded with a World Series triumph in 2004.

It was a couple of hours before the gates to the ballpark opened, so I walked to the Gateway Arch and took the inside tram to the viewing area at the top. With wall-to-wall people mulling around the confined quarters, I returned to the base within five minutes. I eventually worked my way back to the ballpark as the gates opened at 5:30. Such an early entry was reminiscent of all those times my son and I "dragged" the rest of our family to baseball games during our vacations when we were always among the first to enter and last to leave! I vividly recalled a night game in Montreal in June 1970. Steve and I wanted to be at the ballpark when it opened to see as much of the players and field practice as possible. At 5 o'clock, Loretta, Cher, Chris, Steve, and I entered Jerry Park and we didn't leave until the sixteen-inning marathon ended at 2:00 a.m. (and we still had to catch the subway back to our hotel)!

At Busch Stadium I was seated a few rows behind the third base dugout and had superb views of all the field action. Despite a 7-to-1 Red Sox defeat, it was an excellent spectator game shared with a capacity crowd of Cardinal and Red Sox fans full of exemplary enthusiasm and camaraderie. This was baseball at its best.

The next morning I returned to Gateway Arch, this time to its lower level, which housed the Western Movement Museum. A detailed timeline of events from 1800 to 1899 was a veritable encyclopedia of 19th-century America. In another part of the museum, and of special meaning to me, was the chronology of Lewis and Clark's journey told with murals supplemented with the personal, written accounts of Merewether Lewis, William Clark, and other members of the Corps of Discovery. Their adventure was accentuated by an IMAX movie vividly recreating the expedition's route amid the spectacular scenery of today's America; I could almost feel I was accompanying them. As I marveled at their story and the scenes, my emotions got the better of me when I realized I had just driven and/or hiked these special places, sometimes following the very pathways of the great explorers. So much extraordinary beauty to behold and history to be traced -- and I had been there, done it, and enjoyed all of it!

Then suddenly, with no forethought or prior hints, I concluded that *my* journey had ended. Right then and there! I had come full circle. Yes, there were still over fifteen hundred miles to "home," so the trip itself had to continue to its geographical end. But the essence of my odyssey had been fulfilled. I was no longer interested in visiting other landmarks or sites between St. Louis and Connecticut. I realized that in the span of twenty-four hours I had visited one of the premier memorials of Americana, the Lincoln Museum; saw my Red Sox play their longtime National League arch rivals; and visited the site where Meriwether Lewis and William Clark began and ended their historic journey. Given the influential role their trip played in my personal journey of discovery, it felt right to end mine there as well. In my mind, and especially in my heart, I knew my wayward journey was finished.

It took me another eight days to get back to Connecticut and Rhode Island and that included a final night of camping at the Chain-of-Lakes State Park outside Fort Wayne, IN. During my earlier years in business, this area was the center of the diamond die (wire drawing) industry and I often visited customers for our diamond-polishing powders. From there I visited some very dear relatives from my mother's side of our family who lived just outside Detroit.

While there I toured the Henry Ford Museum Complex in Dearborn, which was an incredibly detailed journey through the history of American industry. The collection included all manner and size of machinery and transport vehicles from locomotives to tractors. On display was the bus from which Civil Right's heroine Rosa Parks was arrested after refusing to give up her seat. Also nearby was the chair in which President Lincoln was seated at Ford Theater at the time of his assassination!

It was a hot June day as I left Sterling Heights for Erie, PA, and a popular bird-watching spot, Presque Isle State Park, along the south shore of Lake Erie. With numerous beaches in the park and schools out for the summer, the sun-worshipping crowd was there in full force. After a brief swim and siesta, I left the park and continued into New York State, ultimately arriving in Cooperstown, home to the Baseball Hall of Fame.

This was a sentimental stop for me since Cooperstown has always been a special place for Steve and me to spend time together. As early as I can recall, as so often is the case with fathers and sons, baseball was the common denominator between us. We both played the game and followed the triumphs and travails of major league teams along the way. To this day baseball, and all it encompasses, retains its role as a bonding agent to our relationship. It has provided us a physical forum (the ballpark) for father and son to share common interests and subject matter (baseball) for discussions of people, leadership, and human interactions in a myriad of situations. I have learned much about Steve to love and admire through these shared experiences.

I stayed for a couple of days and completed my journal entries while relaxing poolside at the *Otsego Inn*, situated on the shores of beautiful Lake Otsego. Here I encapsulated the thoughts and emotions of my 170-day odyssey from Watch Hill, RI, to St. Louis, MO…and what a journey it was!

Fig. 38 - Overnight accommodations varied along the route

Epilogue

The memorable words of Walt Whitman's "Song of the Open Road" (from which I quoted at the beginning of this journal) express much of what my journey was about as I traversed America and experienced this country's landscape, culture, and residents. It is truly my good fortune to have been able to travel twenty-thousand miles through thirty-eight states during a six-month period of minimal tourist activity. As a lone traveler, I had an opportunity to see a great deal within a limited time and, most importantly, to engage others, one on one, to better understand what I had seen. Popular national parks such as Yellowstone, Yosemite, and Zion revealed their beauty as I was able to hike the trails and experience these magnificent natural wonders without the hoards of summer visitors.

An important point and one that may be useful to the reader concerns my frequent reference to an aversion to crowds of people, and it deserves clarification. Lest I appear anti-social, it should be noted that many of my most memorable moments along the way involved interaction with other people. Witness my personalized tour of Okefenokee Swamp, Hampton Place, Montgomery, Vicksburg Battlefield, Crowe Agency, fishing the Little Big Horn, to name a few. However, such experiences were often made possible simply because I was a lone visitor.

Similarly, in popular tourist attractions like our national parks, experiencing their unique flavor with minimum crowds can make a huge difference. For instance, the "buffalo jam" that amused me in Yellowstone with only a half- dozen vehicles would have taken on a much different aura were I lined up in July with perhaps a hundred other cars and trailers waiting for hours to traverse a mile of roadway while the buffalo meandered along. A summertime search for lodging outside Yosemite because the park's campgrounds were full would have to detract from a visit there. While watching the Red Sox/Cardinals baseball game was thrilling with over 50,000 people in attendance, crowds would not have been appreciated in other venues. I think you get the picture.

A notable downside to traveling alone is exposure to the potential dangers of hiking in natural wilderness areas. My hikes in Yellowstone's grizzly-bear territory, for instance, armed only with bear bells and pepper spray may not have been particularly responsible decisions. Thankfully, I was blessed with good health, good luck, and abundant energy throughout my journey; I was pleased with my ability to handle sometimes difficult and lengthy hikes and other physical activities. I am also comforted by my resolve to maintain a healthy dietary regimen (notwithstanding several days of fried oysters in the South and beef throughout the West)!

Major themes and cultural issues that particularly imprinted themselves on my memory include the stunning visual beauty, vastness, and geological variety of the western states. The mental images I retain powerfully validate the words of our country's eloquent song, "America the Beautiful." On the other hand, I am troubled by the issues surrounding slavery, the Civil War, and Negroes in America. The intolerable cruelty to which blacks were subjected in pre-Civil War America became sadly clear during my southern sojourn. During the height of slavery in 1860, one-seventh of our population, or four-million blacks and other minorities, were held in bondage.

Another sad chapter in our country's history that came to the forefront for me was the treatment of Native Americans by our government and its military arm, especially during the 19th century. I can't pretend to have any deep understanding of the American Indian issues as they once were and as they continue to play out in our society, but questions do arise as to why we have not done more to rectify the wrongs perpetrated on these Native Americans.

I believe my exposure to these unfortunate episodes in our rich history will make me more sensitive to the circumstances and needs of others. It is my hope that my attitude and conduct toward them will reflect increased empathy, understanding, and good fellowship. On balance, my interaction with people across our country was pleasant, inspirational, and rewarding and I am grateful to call the United States of America my home.

During the course of my travels, I was constantly queried by people I met along the way about the scope and purpose of my journey. Their fascination with, and admiration of, the comprehensiveness of my itinerary left me with a quiet sense of pride and accomplishment. I suspect my odyssey was special to others as well -- acquaintances, friends, family, and especially my late mom, who vicariously accompanied me on my journey. Rather than quell my travel bug, this odyssey of mine only stimulated my desire to pursue additional global adventures on a regular basis.

In closing I return to those questions outlined at the beginning of this book. My time and solitude on the journey provided me the opportunity to introspectively look at my life and its relevance to my family and what I wish to share with them.

1) If you were on your deathbed and wanted to tell your children or the young people to whom you are close the three most important things you have learned in life, what would they be?

a) The freeing power of forgiveness: it enables you to unshackle the wrongs locked in your past. It is love's revolution against unfairness. Only you are the loser by harboring an unforgiving mind.

b) The capacity of ordinary people to achieve extraordinary things by having the will, patience, and courage to follow their convictions.

c) The most valuable asset a person can possess is his/her integrity. Develop, nurture, and preserve it.

2) What gives you the greatest joy, satisfaction, and renewal in your life?

Reflecting on my life to date, I conclude that my most gratifying experiences have come from giving to others.

My odyssey provided me a forum for continued growth, an appreciation for life, and a desire to be a better person.

3) Who are you without your job, your money?

Having removed myself from active full-time employment several years ago, I am still the same person, perhaps with a less competitive edge in my pursuits. Money or lack thereof has never driven my basic behavior. In that regard, I believe I can adapt to varying economic circumstances and remain fundamentally unchanged by them.

4) What activities could you add to your life that would be a source of richness and joy?

The knowledge and insights gained from travel and interactions with peoples of the world continue to excite me. Sharing these experiences with my family and others to enrich and stimulate their minds means much to me. It will be giving of my time, experiences, and possessions that will afford me ultimate happiness.

5) Think of someone you deeply admire, and why.

With all due respect to family members past and present, I think of my sister Doris, who along with her other attributes gives of herself with a generosity and anonymity of unparalleled unselfishness.

As to my future, I know not what paths await me, but the words of author, Jack London, may say it best for how I'd prefer to travel that road:

"I would rather be ashes than dust. I would rather that my spark burn out in a brilliant blaze than it should be stifled by dry-rot. I would rather be a superb meteor, every atom of me in magnificent glow, than a sleepy and permanent planet. The proper function of man is to live, not to exist. I shall not waste my days trying to prolong them. I shall use my time."

This odyssey of mine is really a story about connecting.....with God, myself, my family, friends, and the people I met (past and present) along the way.

Acknowledgements

This book is based on a daily journal fastidiously maintained during the course of my six- month odyssey. That journal was intended to provide a chronological account of the people, places, and events along the way, essentially a legacy to my family and exclusively for their readership. However, after my notes and audio tapes were transcribed, I was advised that there was a worthwhile story to tell and it was suggested that I refine and personalize it. Samuel Coale, professor of American Literature at Wheaton College and book reviewer for *The Providence Journal,* was especially encouraging, but he mandated that I "not remain aloof" and "dig in, dig down with more concrete images and insights. You've got a great arc of a journey here; now fill in the details more candidly, concretely. And you're on your way!" Thank you Sam.

My biggest stumbling block was a personal one. I was hesitant to share myself and my innermost feelings with the outside world. It was ultimately the words of my valued editorial consultant, David Panciera, who pragmatically noted: "Frankly, you have maintained a deep cloak of privacy. No sense in bequeathing a guardedly private legacy. Sort of an oxymoron, don't you think?" His wise counsel prevailed. David also challenged me to provide better clarity, completeness, and detail to my story. The consistency of grammar, punctuation, and terminology is the work of Jane Roderick, a professional editor. There were several reprimands from Jane along the way, but her persistence and tolerance of my deficiencies are noteworthy and I remain most grateful for her contributions. Also, not to be underestimated is the candid, critical review of my early drafts by my good friend Bob Richins. My writings and supporting materials were effectively transposed into finished Word documents by Kevin Corina whose computer skills and timely efforts were invaluable in allowing me to present a quality product to the publisher.

I am truly thankful to the many people with whom I interacted along the way who significantly added to the richness of my experience.

Finally, and most importantly, I am profoundly grateful to my children, my sister, and especially my mother for their unfailing support and encouragement of my decision to embark on a journey of unknown duration as a lone, wayward traveler.

.

www.ingramcontent.com/pod-product-compliance
Lightning Source LLC
Chambersburg PA
CBHW061407280526
45784CB00001B/401